Best Advice

Best Advice

*Wisdom on Ministry
from 30 Leading Pastors
and Preachers*

Edited by William J. Carl III

WESTMINSTER
JOHN KNOX PRESS
LOUISVILLE · KENTUCKY

First edition
Westminster John Knox Press
Louisville, Kentucky

09 10 11 12 13 14 15 16 17 18—10 9 8 7 6 5 4 3 2 1

Scripture quotations from the New Revised Standard Version of the Bible are copyright © 1989 by the Division of Christian Education of the National Council of the Churches of Christ in the U.S.A. and are used by permission.

Book design by Sharon Adams
Cover design by designpointinc.com

Library of Congress Cataloging-in-Publication Data

Best advice : wisdom on ministry from 30 leading pastors and preachers / William J. Carl III, editor.—1st ed.
    p. cm.
Includes bibliographical references.
ISBN 978-0-664-23243-6 (alk. paper)
1. Pastoral theology.   2. Preaching.   I. Carl, William J.
BV4011.3.W57   2009
253—dc22

2008027989

PRINTED IN THE UNITED STATES OF AMERICA

♾ The paper used in this publication meets the requirements of the American National Standard for Information Sciences—Permanence of Paper for Printed Library Materials, ANSI Z39.48-1992

Westminster John Knox Press advocates the responsible use of our natural resources. The text paper of this book is made from at least 30% post-consumer waste.

This book is dedicated to my siblings and their spouses,
Evelyn and Carl Thompson,
Stephen and Karen Carl,
Debbie and Jim Freeman,
who are wonderful teachers, pastors, preachers,
and great models for ministry.

Contents

Preface

Imagine hosting a dinner party where you get to invite distinctive leaders in your field of interest. Most are seasoned veterans, while some are up-and-coming stars, but you get to do the choosing. That was my joyous privilege when Don McKim asked me to edit this wonderful book. The invitations went out and, to my surprise, the acceptances came in quickly. The distinguished invitees were delighted to participate in this feast of pastoral and homiletical fare.

I am especially pleased with the diversity of voices gathered around this table, where the quality of the cuisine is only enhanced by the content of the conversation. Some of the authors have focused on preaching, others on pastoral leadership, while the rest have commented on both.

Knowing how long some of us have been laboring in the vineyard, I calculated that you have before you over a thousand years of cumulative experience.

Now with great joy I invite you to share in the feast you will find in this book. Taste and sample it at your own pace. It may be more than you can digest at one sitting, for this smorgasbord of pastoral and homiletical wisdom is much more than a casual buffet. Take your time with it. Savor it and enjoy it.

Welcome to the banquet! May it be a blessing to your life and your ministry for decades to come.

William J. Carl III
Pittsburgh, Pennsylvania

1

What I Would Like to Tell
My Colleagues in Ministry

JOANNA M. ADAMS

I would love to remind my colleagues about the life-giving
power of the Holy Spirit, the unfailing promises of God,
and the good news of Jesus Christ. Almost thirty years
ago, I committed my life to these spiritual realities as I knelt on the
sanctuary floor, had hands laid upon me, and received the peculiar
office of minister of Word and Sacrament. The most important thing
I have learned since that glorious ordination day is that *we minister,
as we live, by grace*. What follows are a few other insights I have
picked up along the way.

Ministry is more difficult than I thought it would be and harder than
I imagined when I was ordained. My first Sunday at the downtown
church to which I was called fresh out of seminary was Pentecost Sunday. I had purchased a red dress for the occasion. After worship, a
lovely reception was held in the fellowship hall, complete with cucum-
ber sandwiches, cheese straws, and lime sherbet punch. I was thoroughly enjoying meeting my new friends when an elder tapped me on
the shoulder. "There are some people over there who need to speak
to you." I looked across the room, and standing at the foot of the steps
were two of the saddest looking people I had ever seen.

My first reaction, which makes me feel ashamed even today, was
"Who invited them to this nice party?" I got hold of myself and walked

across the room in their direction. They turned out to be the first of many homeless people I would meet, a couple loaded with mental disabilities, plagued by bad luck, and without a friend in the world. The elder and I spent the afternoon trying to locate a place for them to stay the night, but there was no place in the city where a couple could find shelter together for the night. We finally took the man to the men's mission and the woman to the women's mission. They cried when they said goodbye to one another.

I learned that day that Jesus often comes in the person of the stranger. He stands at the door and knocks. When we let him in, we are changed forever as the elder and I were that Pentecost Sunday long ago. Our church went on to become a leader in both advocacy and compassion on behalf of the least, the left-out, and the forgotten. I learned early on that welcoming our Lord and following his way would be demanding. I found myself standing before the city council begging for public toilets. I lost many a night's sleep while staying at the shelter we opened for our homeless friends.

As those early months turned into years, I sometimes found my eyes filling with tears as I invited the congregation to the Lord's Table with the words, "Come unto me all you that are weary and are carrying heavy burdens and I will give you rest. Take my yoke upon you, and learn from me; for I am gentle and humble in heart, and I will give you rest." Jesus was the stranger at the door. He was the host at the table. He was everywhere the giver of grace.

Ministry is more joyful and meaningful than I had ever imagined. What other vocation requires a person to spend time each week studying and wrestling with God's Word, which, over time and with the aid of the Spirit, genuinely reshapes the way you understand God, other people, and yourself? I have always loved the story Walter Wink tells about the woman who walked around her small village with the Bible held high over her head. "Why do you carry that same book every day? There are so many others you could read," she was asked. "Yes, there are," she answered, "but this is the only book that reads me."

What a profound privilege it is to preach most Sundays. Of course, the feelings of fear and inadequacy show up on a regular basis, but then there are those times when I cannot wait to offer the gifts God has given me in the service of God's plan of redemption and renewal for the whole creation. Does it get any better than that? I wish there were better ways to know whether or not my preaching has been effective in ushering people into an awareness of the presence of God. The very sermon I struggled and sweated and chewed my pencil eraser over turns out to be the one somebody writes me a note about, saying, "Thank you for just the word I needed to hear today."

The same is true in ministry. What I have found to be most satisfying are those quiet pastoral encounters that no one other than the person or people involved even know about, but in which I sense that God has allowed me to be a vessel of hope, a flesh-and-blood representative of divine love.

The bigger signs of success, such as the completion of capital campaigns and the growing number of names on the roll, seem less and less important as time goes by. What matters more are the human connections, the moments of laughter, the times of tears, the privilege of holding the babies by the baptismal font, the awesome mystery that surrounds the sacrament of the Lord's Supper, the soul-deep thrill that comes with discovering new and effective ways to serve God and neighbor.

What matters more are the mustard seeds that get planted by hope-filled people who have confidence that God will give the growth. The greatest joy of ministry is seeing what God will do when the people of God are willing to act in faith. From those early church shelters grew more shelters, more advocacy groups, more feeding programs, more affordable housing programs, more day care centers, and more job training programs.

My first solo flight into the pulpit was not my finest hour, homiletically speaking, but at least the word got through to me. The congregations I have served have, in different ways, trusted that God could take their seemingly inconsequential offerings and do great things with them.

Ministry, at its core, is a matter of faith, hope, and love. Faith because, regardless of whether or not my own personal faith is soaring or sinking on any given day, the faith of the church across the ages holds steady, and the faithfulness of God never wavers. I have discovered that churches and church members whose taproot goes down deep into the gospel of Christ always have what it takes, not only to survive but to live abundant lives, rich in service, no matter how daunting the circumstances they are facing.

Hope because, regardless of immediate prospects, the future is in God's hands. How does the hymn put it? "The Lord has promised good to me, His word my hope secures." I have discovered that if you offer people just one-tenth of one ounce of hope, they can do just about anything. In recent years, I have had the privilege of helping a once dying church come back to life and set out to serve Christ in the world in new and vital ways. The secret is hope, grounded in the promise of the One who said, "See, I am making all things new" (Rev. 21:5)

Love because ministry requires the endurance of a lot of things I could have lived forever without. The bias against women in positions of authority in the church, most often hidden but no less real these days, comes to mind. The father of a bride once told me after his daughter's wedding that as soon as the honeymoon was over, there would be another ceremony in the family's home church, because he didn't believe a wedding presided over by a woman "would take."

Love because there are plenty of things to become irritable or resentful about, but neither irritability nor resentment has ever done a thing to serve the purposes of God. Over the years, I have lost what stomach I ever had for ecclesiastical combat, though the issues of inclusion remain of vital importance to me and to our church. I think of how Martin Luther King Jr., after the Montgomery bus boycott and the U.S. Supreme Court decision that ensured victory for his side, told the congregation at the Holt Street Baptist Church: "We have before us the glorious opportunity to inject a new dimension of love into the veins of our civilization. . . . There is still a voice crying out in terms that echo across the generations, saying, 'Love your enemies, bless them that curse you, pray for them that despitefully use you, that you may be children of your Father which is in heaven.'"[1]

The apostle Paul tells us that of all things, only love will last. I am not saying that love is easy, but I do say to every person who has ever asked me for advice as he or she begins a new ministry with a congregation that love is the key: "You must love the congregation as it actually is now, not as you see it one year or five years from now. You must get to know the people and love them each and all as they actually are, not as the people you want them to become after they have been transformed by your brilliant pastoral work and spell-binding preaching. Only after you have lived together in love can you move forward together in hope."

I sometimes think of how poor Moses had to take all the Hebrew people with him through the wilderness. All of them. There must have been days when he didn't like them and days when they didn't like him. There were probably some who were not likeable any of the time, and Moses was surely not likeable all the time. Across the years, I have taken comfort in Frederick Buechner's reminder that "love is not primarily an emotion but an act of will."[2] Sometimes, of course, love is more than that. To love and be loved as a pastor by the people is a gift beyond measure. Even when I have let them down or somehow failed them, the people have gone with me all the way. When they have let me down, I have never stopped loving them or failed to remember that we are all sinners, saved by grace.

Know your place. By that, I mean that a minister must respect the particular context of the congregation he or she serves. I have pastored in five different parishes. Each has had its own culture, its own way of worship, its own way of reaching out to the community, and its own way of being community. You cannot transfer good ideas from place to place as if they were fungible commodities. Ask your new church to receive you as a novice, and let them teach you how to lead them.

What I would most like to tell my colleagues in ministry is not to make the mistakes I have made, but we all know that won't do much good. For the most part, my mistakes have revolved around my tendency not to respect my human limits. Put another way, I have not known when to quit. I work on a sermon until I stand up to preach it, and then I will leave out parts of the manuscript as I substitute an idea or an illustration that comes to me as I speak.

I often work too many hours, though I was wisely warned against it by a colleague on the ministerial staff at my second church. "When are you going home? Don't you know only the devil works seven days a week?" Over the years, I have learned the necessity of setting limits and live within them more than I used to. I have learned that if I take up all the room, there is no room for the Spirit to inspire, or for the people to be empowered. These days, I pay more attention to messages my body sends me. I pay more attention to my life and to the rich and abundant life I share with family and friends. I don't take myself as seriously as I used to, even as I take ministry more seriously than ever. Never has the world been more in need of hearing the ever fresh, always relevant story of Jesus and his love.

Finally, I take comfort in Paul's reassurance that "we have this treasure in clay jars, so that it might be made clear this extraordinary power belongs to God and does not come from us" (2 Cor. 4:7). There are a lot worse things to be in life than one of God's clay jars—cracks, lumps, and all.

Notes

1. Quoted in Charles Marsh, *The Beloved Community* (New York: Basic Books, 2005), 1.
2. Frederick Buechner, *Wishful Thinking* (New York: Harper and Row, 1973), 54.

2

Listen to What the Congregation Says about Preaching

RONALD J. ALLEN

L istening is fundamental to preaching. Books, conferences, and classes in seminary and continuing education urge preachers to listen to:

- what a biblical text, Christian doctrine, or practice invites the congregation to believe and do;
- the context of the congregation—the culture, issues, feelings, and other dynamics at work in both the congregation and in the larger social world;
- their own personal and social experience—their history, what is happening to them in the moment, their own hopes and fears and questions; and
- other sources of insight (such as philosophy, the arts, political analysis, sociology, and psychology).

Over the last decades, some leaders in the field of preaching have encouraged preachers to invite members of the congregation into sermon preparation itself. John S. McClure, for instance, uses the image of a roundtable discussion to advocate a process of collaborative preaching. Preachers bring together a group of laity the week before the sermon to help identify how issues related to the biblical texts are important to them.[1] Some preachers now sponsor such feed-forward groups on a weekly basis.

Listen to What the Congregation Says about Preaching

I applaud these and other such efforts while pointing to an additional way that the preacher can listen to the congregation: Listening to what *the congregation says about preaching* can help ministers more deeply understand the context in which they preach so they can develop sermons that will engage the congregation. Such listening can also help a pastor come to a more penetrating understanding of other aspects of congregational culture.

This discovery began when I noticed an odd situation in the preaching world. The sermon is prepared for the congregation, but very few books, articles, speeches, and workshops that seek to help preachers develop sermons draw on what listeners themselves report as engaging (or disengaging) when they hear sermons. Most approaches to preaching are based on a particular theological point of view (e.g., Barth) or approach to philosophy, on communication theory, on different modes of literary analysis, or on the anecdotal experience of ministers. My initial scholarly work in preaching, for instance, used Susanne K. Langer's philosophy of art, with its focus on the arts (including texts) and expressions of feeling as a way to understand biblical passages, hermeneutics, and preaching. When the literature of preaching takes a turn toward the listener, it tends to rely upon what the preacher observes about the listeners rather than on what the listeners report.

A few years ago, Christian Theological Seminary received a grant from the Lilly Endowment to interview people who regularly listen to sermons asking them to identify the qualities that draw them into preaching and those that do not. Guided by a board of professors of preaching, I served as director, with Mary Alice Mulligan as associate director. We talked with 263 people in 28 congregations—nine composed primarily of people of African American origin, sixteen of people largely of European origin, and three that were mixed along racial-ethnic lines. The congregations, located in the Midwest, were drawn from twelve historic African Methodist and European denominations such as the African Methodist Episcopal Church, various Baptist bodies, the Christian Church (Disciples of Christ), the Mennonite Church, and the United Methodist Church. About half of the listeners were interviewed individually and about half in small groups. The interviews lasted an hour to an hour and a half.

The interview questions were organized around four themes adapted from Aristotle's categories of rhetorical appeals. Interviewees were asked how they perceived themselves to be engaged (1) by the *ideas* of the sermon (logos), (2) by *feelings* stirred by the sermon (pathos), (3) by their perception of the *character* of the preacher and by their *sense of relationship* with the preacher (ethos), and (4) by the *embodiment* or delivery of the sermon. Rather than ask the interviewees to talk about a sermon they had just heard, we asked a series of questions that invited the listeners to draw on their long experiences in listening to sermons and to give specific examples.

The biggest surprise to me was in how very important preaching is to most of these congregants. When asked, "What would be missing if there were no sermon in the service of worship?" several people answered flatly, "Me." Dozens of others said that they count on the sermon to help them discern and respond to God's presence and purposes. The sermon is a key to helping them determine who they are and what they are to do.[2] I have long thought that congregations value preaching, but these respondents intensified that conviction. Walking away from this data, one can only conclude that preaching deserves a preacher's best time and attention.

Many of the nuts-and-bolts things that we learned are set forth in four books:

- *Make the Word Come Alive: Lessons from Laity* identifies the twelve most common qualities that interviewees seek in sermons. These range from "helping us figure out what God wants" to "talking loud enough so that we can hear."[3]
- *Hearing the Sermon: Relationship, Content, and Feeling* not only looks in detail at how a sense of relationship with the preacher, the argument of the sermon, and feeling contribute to a listener's willingness to take the sermon seriously, but presents the discovery that most listeners enter the sermon through one of these settings.[4]

- *Believing in Preaching: What Listeners Hear in Sermons* identifies diverse clusters of listener perception in regard to ten major issues in preaching from the purpose of the sermon through authority and the Bible to sermons on controversial subjects and how preaching shapes the congregation as community. There are some surprises here. For example, listeners *want* the preacher to offer theological interpretation on many hot-button topics.[5]
- *Listening to Listeners: Homiletical Case Studies* looks in detail at the transcripts of six interviews, from five individuals (two African Americans and three persons of European origin, three women and two men) and a small group that is racially mixed. Annotations highlight what we can learn about preaching from these listeners.[6]

Beyond the insights about preaching and listening that are specific to the interviews and books, the study reinforces the fact that each congregation is its own listening culture. Consequently, a preacher cannot simply take the discoveries, principles, and conclusions that are articulated in these books and apply them in the same way in New York City; Bean Blossom, Indiana; Wichita, Kansas; Maryville, Tennessee; or Bend, Oregon. In order to understand the listening climate of the local congregation, the preacher needs to listen to listeners in that congregation.

Strategies for Listening to the Congregation

A preacher has multiple options for identifying a congregation's perceptions of preaching. In most congregations, an optimum way for the preacher to discover what listeners value in preaching is to have interviews conducted with individuals and with small groups in the congregation.[7]

Our study suggests that the interviews typically should focus on the listeners' perceptions of preaching over the course of their listening lives more than on the specific preaching of the current minister. Some congregants are reluctant to comment directly on the preaching of their current pastor. Of course, when illustrating their responses, listeners will often cite particular sermons from their current pastor.

The interviews should usually be conducted not by the preacher but by another interviewer. Many listeners are hesitant to speak freely to the preacher, whereas they are quite open in their comments to other interviewers. The local preacher can call upon an outside party (such as a neighboring minister or a social worker) to conduct interviews. The interviewers can summarize listener comments for the preacher.

Of course, as trust develops between preacher and people, it may be possible for the local preacher to conduct some interviews, especially with small groups. Again, listeners are often more likely to talk honestly if the minister asks questions about preaching in general rather than about her own sermons.

At the beginning of the interview process, questions might be adapted from the ones we used in the study. A preacher might refine these questions or create others more suitable to the context in conversation with a small group from the congregation or with a minister or with a colleague group. In any event, the questions should be open-ended so as to give the interviewees an opportunity to fill out their responses with rich detail.

The following samples illustrate the larger body of questions we used in the original interviews. The associated rhetorical category precedes each question.

- (Logos) What do you think your pastor is doing when he or she preaches?
- (Logos) When does a sermon have authority for you?
- (Pathos) Can you tell me about a sermon that stirred your emotions?
- (Pathos) What in that sermon stirred you? (This question is a follow-up to the preceding one.)
- (Ethos) Talk a little bit about your relationship with the preachers that you have had.
- (Embodiment) Would you please describe for me a preacher whose physical presence in the pulpit was really good—whose delivery was really engaging?
- (General closing question) If you had one or two things you could tell preachers that would help them energize you when you are listening to a sermon, what would they be? (This question often generated some of the most revealing responses.)[8]

Of course, preachers can reflect alone on the data that is gathered through the interviews, but the board of our "listener study" project found that our understanding of the interviews deepened and broadened when we worked together. A preacher might process the data with clergy colleagues, with a group from the congregation, or with someone who teaches preaching at a nearby seminary or who teaches speech at the local college.

The preacher and others want to pay attention to what the interviewees find to be engaging when hearing sermons. In what ways does the preacher's present approach to preaching manifest such qualities? Are there points at which the minister's current approach to preaching manifests characteristics that listeners find disengaging? If so, in what ways can the preacher become more engaging?

Another approach might be for a small group of listeners and the preacher to read one of the books from the listener study and to reflect their own viewpoint. For instance, as noted above, *Make the Word Come Alive* identifies twelve qualities in preaching that were important to the study group. To what degree does the small group concur? What would they add? Where do they differ?

Closing Cautions

The intent here is not to license the preacher to give the congregation what they want to hear. The preacher's vocation is to help the congregation adequately interpret God's presence and purposes and to respond faithfully. Indeed, the preacher's deepest theological convictions may run against the grain of what listeners perceive to be engaging. The purpose of interviewing is to help preachers become sensitive to ways in which they can shape sermons with theological integrity so that the congregation has optimum opportunities to engage the gospel and its claims.

I do not wish to leave the impression that listeners want ministers to change their approaches to preaching in ways that violate the integrity of the personhood of the preacher. To the contrary, the listeners in our study repeatedly stress that they respect preachers who are themselves in the pulpit with respect to what they say (intellectual honesty) and to the way in which they say it (in language and embodiment). Indeed, these listeners are suspicious of preachers who assume a different persona in the pulpit than in their everyday behavior. However, the listeners are also clear that most preachers can change aspects of their preaching in ways that can improve communication without violating homiletical integrity.

I have been surprised at how much I have learned from listening to listeners. Indeed, when it comes to preaching, I now regard listeners as some of my most important teachers.

Notes

1. John S. McClure, *The Roundtable Pulpit: Where Leadership and Preaching Meet* (Nashville: Abingdon Press, 1995).
2. The sermon does not carry this burden alone. For an exploration of how the congregation functions as a system, see Ronald J. Allen, *Preaching and Practical Ministry*, Preaching and Its Partners (St. Louis: Chalice Press, 2000).
3. Mary Alice Mulligan and Ronald Allen, *Make the Word Come Alive: Lessons from Laity* (St. Louis: Chalice Press, 2005).
4. Ronald Allen, *Hearing the Sermon: Relationship, Content, and Feeling* (St. Louis: Chalice Press, 2004).
5. Mary Alice Mulligan, Diane Turner-Sharazz, Dawn Ottoni Wilhelm, and Ronald Allen, *Believing in Preaching: What Listeners Hear in Sermons* (St. Louis: Chalice Press, 2005).
6. John S. McClure, Ronald Allen, Dale P. Andrews, L. Susan Bond, Dan P. Moseley, and G. Lee Ramsey Jr., *Listening to Listeners: Homiletical Case Studies* (St. Louis: Chalice Press, 2004).
7. For more detailed suggestions regarding interviewing, see ibid., 141–64.
8. The full set of questions is available in Allen, *Hearing the Sermon*, 135–36, and in McClure et al., *Listening to Listeners*, 181–82.

3

Three Temptations of the Pastor

CRAIG BARNES

No one goes to seminary to service complaints, manage a relentlessly demanding nonprofit organization, or enter the fray of local church politics. But every pastor is tempted to use up most of the day wandering around in these soul-consuming diversions. When that happens, it feels like you're stuck in a circle of Dante's *Inferno* and can't figure out how to get free. This isn't what you signed up to do. You were ordained to Word and Sacrament, which means you were called to enter every circle of your congregation's life, including the hellish ones, with a devotion to finding and then proclaiming God's Word.

There is a legion of temptations to stray from this true calling, but the most seductive distractions can be found in the three temptations Jesus faced in the desert. As in our time, they were all temptations that would have derailed Jesus' mission to be the Word and the sacrament of God's grace on earth.

All three of these great temptations occurred immediately after Jesus' baptism when the heavens opened and a voice proclaimed, "This is my son, the Beloved, with whom I am well pleased" (Matt. 3:17). Note that Jesus did not receive this designation until he submitted to John's baptism for sinners. The one who knew no sin identified with us in this baptism. This is another revelation of the incarnation, and it is why the dove of the Holy Spirit descended upon Jesus as he came out of the waters.[1] When the Son of God finds us at the shores of the Jordan and identifies with us, the identification is so complete that we have to hear heaven's proclamation as applying to all humanity. We too are the beloved of God. That's not because we deserve to be the beloved or finally found a way to wash away our own sins. It's because we have all been found, brought home, and adopted into the Son's beloved relationship with the Father.

Proclaiming this extraordinary news in the pulpit, counseling session, hospital room, and even the committee meeting is at the core of the pastor's calling. Everything else is distraction.

The Temptation to Be Full

The first and perhaps most basic temptation is to take away deep hunger. The devil began this first temptation with the words, "If you are the son of God . . ." In other words, if we are really so beloved, the devil reasons, we should not be hungry. Few things are more tempting to pastors than to relieve the hunger of their parishioners.

We were created as a hungry people. Every morning one of the first things we confront is appetite. We hunger not only for food but also for intimacy and friendship, power and security, health and freedom from pain. No matter how much we consume, we are never full for long. The hunger just keeps returning. It's supposed to.

Our insatiable hunger confronts us with a choice. Will we believe in our appetite, or will we choose to have faith in the faithfulness of God? This choice is how God honors humans, and it is one of the ways we are distinguished from the rest of creation. We are free to rise above our hunger.

Whenever Jesus healed the sick, exorcised demons, or fed the hungry, the purpose of his miracles was not to satisfy an appetite for food or health. The purpose was to draw people's attention to God's love for them. As Jesus explained to the devil in response to this first temptation, we live not by bread alone but by the word that comes from God. That word had just come down from heaven—"This is my son, the Beloved." But the only worthwhile response to "I love you" is "I love you too." That can only be affirmed as a choice. And only the hungry are free to make that choice.

Of course, one of the reasons we love God is because of the many blessings we have received from God. This is why Jesus taught us to pray, "Give us this day our daily bread" (Matt. 6:11). But if we had all the bread we desired, God would be reduced to a servant that we might appreciate but not really love. As the old theologians often explained, the gutsy form of love emerges in spite of the things God does not do for us. In the words of Job, "Though God slay me, yet will I trust in him" (Job 13:15 KJV). Freely choosing to be faithful, in spite of our hunger, is exactly what it means to love God.

The Grand Inquisitor in Dostoevsky's great novel *The Brothers Karamazov* has long haunted me. In the novel, Jesus returns to the city of Seville in the sixteenth century at the height of the Spanish Inquisition. The Grand Inquisitor, who is an old cardinal of the church with a withered face and sunken eyes, recognizes Jesus and throws him in prison for interrogation. The inquisitor is furious with Jesus for his response to the three temptations:

> You came empty handed with nothing but some vague promises of freedom, which . . . men cannot even conceive and which they fear and dread, for there has never been anything more difficult for man and human society to bear than freedom. . . . In the end they will always lay their freedom at our feet and say to us, "enslave us, but feed us."[2]

It is incredibly tempting for pastors to believe we are fulfilling our calling if we satisfy the hungry complaints within the congregation for something more—more programs, more people, more money, more inspiring worship, and certainly more of the pastor's time. The yearning for more is insatiable, and nothing is more enslaving than a church that promises to keep doing more to fill the created hunger.

The pastor's job is not to offer anything that mitigates more communion with God. Sometimes a new program or change in worship will enhance this experience of sacred love. Often it will only distract everyone, including the pastor, from the reminder that it is for God alone that we hunger. Another new youth director really won't do.

The Temptation to Be Certain

The devil then took Jesus to the top of the temple in Jerusalem and said, "If you are the Son of God throw yourself down." Then he quotes a pledge from the Psalms that promises angelic protection for the beloved.

We can almost see them on the top of the temple:

"Go on. You do believe you're the beloved of God, don't you?"

"Yes."

"Are you absolutely sure?"

"Yes."

"Well, it seems like you should be willing to prove it. Jump!"

Jesus, who also knows Scripture, reminds the devil that we cannot put God to the test, which ends the temptation.

It may seem to the pastor that it would help parishioners to prove God's love for them. This is what preachers attempt when they use up their sermon trying to remove doubt. But nothing is more deadly to a relationship than having to prove love. For God to send down the angels to take away our doubts would only result in removing our freedom to have faith in the love of God. Like hunger, doubt gives meaning and substance to our choice to live as God's beloved.

For this reason, the sermon shouldn't try to convince as much as to reveal. No one gets argued into the kingdom. All of us are compelled to come home like prodigals who find themselves in the gracious arms of the Father. The preacher's job is simply to reveal that love. Then the memory of the Father's house is rekindled in the pews, and the journey to the outstretched arms is begun again.

The pastor, however, can only reveal as much about God as the Scriptures do. There is a part of the Holy One that will always remain a mysterious, untamable whirlwind. This means we pastors should spend more time with *who* than *why*. Revealing a mysterious, holy lover is hard work, and for that reason the pastor is always tempted to revert back to being a friend of Job with lots of explanations and arguments. If we can prove why some things happen in the lives of our parishioners, the thinking goes, then we can get a leash around God. But whatever it is that we've leashed, it certainly isn't God.

The prophet Isaiah gives thanks that God is hidden (Isa. 45:15). That is because unlike the idols, God cannot be controlled, not even by our systematic theologies. We will always find God at work outside of any intellectually constructed box. That forces us to make choices to believe in a God who is beyond all proofs, which brings us back to faith. And again, faith is the only means by which anyone can maintain love. God will never settle for less with us. So we join the old prophet Isaiah in giving thanks that God is hidden.

Most parishioners have never seen a real miracle in their entire lives. What they have seen are plenty of illustrations of God's love for them. And they have heard the gospel proclamation that they are forgiven and restored to triune communion as heirs of God and joint heirs of Jesus Christ. But this history of divine care and gospel proclamation still makes plenty of room for doubt. Thank God for that.

The congregation needs doubt to make room for faith to emerge. Doubt is not the enemy but the companion of faith. When people stay with their doubt, and press it honestly, in time they may come to doubt their doubt, and choose to believe.

The Temptation to Make a Deal with the Devil

The devil then took Jesus to a very high mountain, showed him all of the kingdoms of the world, and offered to give them to Jesus if Jesus would fall down and worship him. Again, Jesus responds with Scripture: "Away with you, Satan! For it is written, 'Worship the Lord your God and serve only him.'"

Jesus did not say, "Kingdoms of the world? What do I want with them?" That's because Jesus would love to have the kingdoms of the world. So this is not a temptation about ends. It's a temptation about means. The devil isn't trying to convince Jesus to abandon the Messiah business. That wouldn't have tempted Jesus. What was tempting was the devil's offer to help Jesus with his own goals of returning the beloved kingdoms of the world to God.

We pastors have high and lofty goals. We went to seminary to proclaim good news, to learn how to speak holy words, to hold trembling hands, and to serve the church. So the devil is never going to tempt us by saying, "Why don't you forget this ministry and start running numbers for the mob?" No, the devil doesn't ask us to give up our holy dreams. He just tells us that we have to get realistic about what those dreams will require. He tells us that we have to make a few compromises with our convictions but that the end will justify the means. He tells us that the world belongs to him, that evil is so much a part of the ecclesiastical system, and that our success necessitates a little complicity with how it is. "If you want to be a successful pastor, you can," he promises. "All you have to do is make a deal with the devil." As soon as the pastor takes that deal, it soon becomes apparent that the cost is the souls of both the pastor and the church.

It seems that these days the devil has some special deals for pastors. Certainly one of these is to work as if Jesus never survived the cross and now it is up to the pastor to take over his work of salvation in the church. Another demonic deal is to reduce the great historic theological tradition to either a conservative or liberal social ideology. Still another is to perceive the pastor as an enterprising entrepreneur who only needs to adopt the latest marketing advice from the business schools. All of these deals will provide temporary encouragement from the kingdoms of the world. None of them will help a single person choose to live in beloved communion with God.

All that the devil could offer Jesus was the "real" world he *saw*. Jesus resisted that temptation because he was committed to the world he *envisioned*—a world beloved. The world has far too many realists and not nearly enough visionaries. The last thing Jesus could be accused of was being a realist. When he claimed to be the Messiah, the Pharisees asked, "Who are you?" Similarly, Gregory the Great, Martin Luther, Martin Luther King Jr., Mother Teresa, and Nelson Mandela were all told that their great dreams were completely unrealistic. Thank God they all refused to be limited by the world they saw and instead chose to live by the ultimate reality of a beloved vision.

This is why the devotional life is so critical to the pastor. It is there, where the pastor draws aside to a lonely place alone with God, that holy dreams are renewed. There the pastor hears the voice from heaven, is restored in the church's identity as the Beloved, and finds the courage to resist the devil's lousy deals.

Notes

1. The Spirit is the agent of the incarnation. Mary conceived because the Spirit came upon her. The Spirit reappeared in Jesus' baptism and then drove him into the wilderness to be tempted as all humans, offering additional testimonies to the incarnation. The Spirit is also the agent of sanctification, adopting us into the triune communion. Thus, the work of the Spirit is to bind Christ to us, and us to Christ.
2. Fyodor Dostoevsky, *The Brothers Karamazov,* trans. Andrew R. MacAndrew (New York: Bantam Books, 1970), 304–5.

4

Toward a Definition of Preaching

DAVID BARTLETT

For many years I began an introductory course in preaching with a lecture called "Toward a Definition of Preaching." The "Toward" part of the title was an acknowledgment that my understanding of the preaching task was always in process. (I did change the lecture a bit from year to year.) Calling the lecture a "Definition of Preaching" seemed more inviting than calling it "Ten Rules for Preaching," especially since the lecture always ended with an almost Lutheran plea to preach gospel instead of law. "Ten Rules for Preaching Grace" seemed almost oxymoronic.

I have not taught that course for several years now, but three marks of the definition seem to me worth highlighting and expanding.

Preaching Is Biblical

The first mark is that *preaching is biblical*. The obvious and still central claim is that the preacher is not first of all a philosopher, social critic, or raconteur but an interpreter of the texts. When I encountered Karl Barth's work in my first year of seminary, he taught me that the word of God comes to us in Christ, then in Scripture, and then in preaching about Christ as we interpret Scripture. Having been convinced of that, I have never turned back.

21

My colleague Robert Wilson has helped me realize that I need to say more. The best way to prepare for biblical preaching is to read the Bible. By that I do not mean just reading Bible passages, and especially I do not mean just reading the Bible passages for next Sunday. I mean reading the Bible, great gobs of it, whole books.

Paul did not know he was writing pericopes; he thought he was writing letters. Matthew, Mark, Luke, and John had no idea that chunks of their Gospels would be assigned for the Third Sunday of Advent or Proper Thirteen. Paul wrote letters that cohere around particular themes and make essential claims, and the evangelists wrote stories that come together only as stories, as narratives with beginning, middle, end, conflict, and confusion.

Both Paul and the evangelists could write their letters or tell their stories only because they were steeped in the rich tradition of the Hebrew Bible, and when you read Paul or the Gospels you realize that they did not just use the Old Testament to proof-text but were immersed in its stories and shaped by its images. When we read the Old Testament more we understand the New Testament better. When we preach Old and New we come closer to preaching the full counsel of God.

Furthermore, along with guides to the lectionary texts, I hope that preachers will make the time to read studies of particular books. Commentaries are best for checking out details, but there are wonderful volumes that provide an overview of what the biblical books are doing overall.

Of course, most of us will preach on pericopes and fragments, but we will preach better if we have a rich sense of the larger context in which these jewels are set. Also, if we have a pretty good idea of what Matthew is up to, for instance, we will not need to revisit that question every three years or every three Sundays.

Preaching Is Personal

The second mark of preaching is that *preaching is personal*—aimed at real and particular persons. All of us who have taught homiletics have shared our standard disclaimer about how our favorite preaching was always that which we did to our own congregations, after which many of my DMin students have suggested that I simply give up tenure and head for one of those appealing parishes with its dubious job security.

Our professorial testimony may be a bit romantic and a lot nostalgic, but it is also partly true. Even on those occasions when I preach four sermons to the same congregation over four weeks, I know them better by the fourth week and begin to preach to *them* as opposed to merely preaching in their presence.

All this is to say that the best personal preaching has to be aware of who the people are. Who is out there? What have they been up to this week? What do they read? What do they watch on television? The sharing of joys and concerns may be especially pertinent for this week's pastoral prayer but also for next week's sermon.

The best way to find this out is to hang out with the people you're preaching to. Attend the youth group meeting and the women's circle meeting and stop doodling on your notepad during the trustees' meeting. Read the novel that one of your parishioners recommended even though its literary quality may not be exactly what you prefer. Look at the local newspaper as well as the *New York Times*. When you've got a question, search the topic on the Web and learn where many of your people are finding their answers. Take a walk through the neighborhood where your people live. Stop, look, and listen.

Paul Holmer, who taught philosophical theology when I was a divinity school student, used to say that when he preached he always did so with one person in mind—not the same person every week, but some particular person. There are some dangers to that. You may make it all too clear to the rest of the congregation just who it is you are talking to and just what it is you are worried about. You may feel deflated if you rev up the sermon with one person in mind and she is off visiting her mother that week.

However, the overall advice is good. When you prepare the sermon envision the faces of those who are apt to be listening. Notice what you are praying for God to do in their lives. Preach toward that.

In the later years of my preaching I have come to realize that part of what makes the persons I preach to distinctive is that they have different ways of hearing, learning, attending. At the simplest level that means that the person who is staring into space may be paying the closest attention, and the person looking straight at me may be noticing only that my tie clashes with my stole.

At a more complicated level, the distinctions in ways of learning mean that some people love stories and learn from them, and other people are narratively challenged but propositionally brilliant. Some preachers think it is our job to turn our congregations into lovers of paradox or fans of poetry. Usually it is job enough for us to help God turn them into Christians. That means that sometimes we will lay aside the kind of preaching we like best, with its three points, and try to tell a real story, or the other way around. I noticed that though most of us in seminaries gave up on three points, lots of listeners love to know just where we are in the sermon and to have a clue or two about how to remember our words for the week ahead. In the ideal world we would probably have a preaching rotation between right-brain and left-brain preachers; in the real world most of us have to jump-start each side of our own brains from time to time.

To say that preaching is personal is to say that we are persons too, and what we say will reflect who we are. We should not use the pulpit as the opportunity to work out our personal problems in the presence of our congregation. Nor should we implicitly plead with them to take care of us, to be our pastors. Those of us in denominations without bishops need to find ad hoc overseers who can be pastors to our need. We talk to them on Thursday so that on Sunday we can preach Christ and not ourselves.

Even more generally, each of us is more interesting to herself than to anyone else. And the older we get, the more impressed we are by our own memories. Of course, there's a danger of talking too much about oneself in preaching. However, there is an equal and opposite danger of seeming disengaged from what should be entirely engaging. The preacher who says he does not want to show too much of himself in a sermon and therefore talks in a monotone about theological abstractions shows a good deal about himself: he is, or appears to be, deliberately distanced from the most vital task in the world. The question is not how often we say "I" or "me" in the sermon. The question is how convinced we are that what we are saying matters—to everybody there that morning, preacher included.

The letters of the apostle Paul are a good example of faithful testimony. They are all about Christ crucified and God, who will be all in all. However, sometimes Paul could also say, "I am not ashamed of the gospel," and the self-reference pointed straight beyond the self.

Sometimes he had to remind his listeners, and maybe himself, that his life was intended to be shaped like the gospel he preached and that God's power was always made perfect in his weakness.

Preaching Is Good News

The lecture "Toward a Definition of Preaching" always heads toward the same goal, however much of it is revised through the years. Preaching is always good news. That does not mean, of course, that preaching is easy news, cheap grace, or prize without pain. Like all real news, preaching must be utterly honest, and that means it will not be consistently pleasant.

Nonetheless, there is a world of difference between saying, "You must love God and neighbor," and saying, "Because God in Christ loves you, you may love God and neighbor." From childhood on we are trained to tune out our parents whenever they begin any sentence with "You must" or "You've got to." In sermons we have found a device that we think gets around this: "Let us love God and the neighbor," but "Let us" still computes as "You must" or "You've got to." When congregations hear "You must" or "let us," they simply stop listening.

I have urged my students to try going through their sermon manuscripts or notes and removing every "You must," "You've got to," "We must," or "Let us." Almost unfailingly, they find that their preaching gets richer. This happens not just because the indicative makes for better communication than the imperative. Their preaching gets richer because our whole enterprise is grounded in the great surprise by which God entered human history with blessing and redemption.

Preaching is always news; it is always good. Why else would we be standing up there doing this odd thing?

5

Why Stay in the Church?

JOHN BUCHANAN

I suppose we've all thought about life outside the church and the ministry at one time or another. What if I had gone to law school instead of seminary, earned an MBA instead of an MDiv, or joined the Marines? I suppose most of us have decided to be a minister not once but many times. In fact, after more than four decades of ministry, I have concluded that the vocational decision, the response to a call—a bolt out of the blue, a voice in the night, a persistent itch we could not scratch—is a decision we make every day.

One of my mentors, Barbara Brown Taylor, who writes and speaks with elegant faithfulness and integrity, wrote a bestseller titled *Leaving Church*.[1] On the book jacket is a picture of a white dove flying out of a bird cage with the door wide open. It is an important book, and the picture on the cover suggests that for Taylor parish ministry had become a kind of captivity, a small cage with no room for flying.

The majority of us choose to stay in, maybe because we can't do anything else for which someone would pay us. More likely, however, we have discovered ways to fly, soar even, in our ministries. I offer here some thoughts about staying alive, healthy, effective, and faithful in ministry.

There are challenges, to say the least. For one thing, there is the church, the institution with its creaky structures, striving to maintain itself in the midst of what feels like a violent upheaval. Many of us spent a fair amount of our preparation for ministry criticizing what we loved to call the "institutional church," as if there were any other kind except in the heart and imagination of God. Then the church ordained us and we threw ourselves into it, serving on committees, attending meetings, rubbing shoulders with people who labored inside the ecclesiastical bureaucracy. We got caught up in the great issues of the day: race, peace, poverty, and now sexual orientation and whether or not gay and lesbian Christians should be ordained. We experienced hostility inside the church and between brothers and sisters who used to be friends. It wore us out and broke our hearts.

Now, to make matters worse, just as the structures are creaking, and we, personally, are depressed about the state of the church, sociologists are telling us that postmodern religion is not only post-denominational but post-Christian. Contemporary Americans are "seekers," not "joiners." Religion is personal, a private journey that has nothing to do with church. The minister meets the important, overarching cultural revolution modestly but regularly in a premarital conference in his or her study. Jennifer introduces Kevin, who says, "I'm not religious, Reverend. I believe in God and all that, but I haven't been in church for years. So I'd like to keep the religious stuff to a minimum in our wedding."

To stay in, we need to learn to forgive the church for being a human institution and church people for being people. We live in the tension between the entity about which we sing, "The church's one foundation is Jesus Christ her Lord. She is his new creation, by water and the word," and the reality of arguing over the color of the carpet and the choice of hymns.

For what it's worth, I think those who stay get to participate in one of the great transitions in Christian history. Frederick Buechner writes, "Maybe the best thing that could happen to the Church would be for some great tidal wave of history to wash it all away—the church buildings tumbling, the church money all lost, the church bulletins blowing through the air like dead leaves, the differences between preachers and congregations all lost too. Then all we would have left would be each other and Christ, which was all there was in the first place."[2] Sometimes it feels like that is exactly what is happening to us. We are approaching a kind of exile. We have lost much of our privilege, entitlement, and authority in postmodernity. Where it all will end God only knows—literally. But what an important and exciting time it is to be part of it.

We should stop blaming others for our predicament—"It's the liberals'/conservatives' fault"—and remember that in spite of our disestablishment, churches are still an important part of the landscape. It is in churches like ours that the world sees a religion unafraid of critical thinking, ready to engage science, the arts, and the great issues of the day. It is in churches that the world occasionally sees a religion of hospitality, grace, and unconditional love, a critical counterpoint to the religion the media loves, a religion of exclusivity and violence. It is in churches that the world sees a radical alternative to the market mentality that reduces everything, even religion, to discovering what religious consumers want. It is in churches like ours that the world occasionally sees a religion that takes God's world seriously, the good but fragile and endangered creation, a religion that refuses to reduce human values to abortion and same-sex marriage, a religion that has not forgotten its own prophetic tradition and continues to witness to a God of justice and peace.

Leading congregations into the future will require women and men who are smart, perceptive students of the new world in which we find ourselves, brave enough to try new things, faithful enough to remember that this venture is not in our hands alone and that even if everything is washed away we still have Christ and his promise that the gates of hell will not prevail against us.

The responsibilities and realities of ministry can be a challenge as well. We live "close to the flames," writes Eileen Lindner, close to the heat and passion and tragedy and exultation, close to the pain and loss and unbelievable joy of human life.[3] People invite us into their lives at a level accessible to no one else and tell us things they tell no one else, things we carry around in our hearts all our lives. They call us when they lose a job or when a spouse dies. They come to tell us that sex is no longer interesting, to announce that they no longer believe in God, that their teenager is doing cocaine. They come to us to bury their dead and marry their children. They want us by their hospital beds when they, or loved ones, are critically ill, and they invite us into that most intimate space of all in human life—the time when it comes to an end.

They tell us they love our preaching so much that we become addicts hooked on postworship compliments, and they devastate us with criticism when we are most vulnerable. They scold us for condemning the war and not condemning the war. They cancel their pledge because of what we said or didn't say about homosexuality. They watch our families and discuss our compensation. They know what kind of car we drive and where we go on vacation.

And—remarkably—they not only let us into their lives and intrude into ours, but they come week after week and sit quietly and listen to us talk. If there is a more astonishing fact and a more unlikely honor than that, I don't know what it might be.

Barbara Brown Taylor says that being a clergyperson "seemed slightly less dicey than being chief engineer at a nuclear plant. In both cases, one needed to know how to approach great power without loosing great danger and getting fried in the process."[4]

And so some thoughts on not getting fried:

Find a mentor. I was thrown into ministry without a single course in practical theology, homiletics, or leadership. I could cite Paul Tillich, but I hadn't the foggiest notion of how to baptize a baby. So I watched ministers who knew how to do it and unconsciously imitated them. While practical academic courses provide an intellectual framework, we learn to do ministry by imitating those who do it well. So find a mentor, then watch and imitate. It's how we learn to preach. We listen to good preachers and read good sermons. Some call it "silent mentoring." Ernie Campbell, at Riverside Church, was my mentor and didn't even know it, didn't know me, for that matter.

Do the most important thing first. At the heart of surviving and loving ministry is time management, and for most of us that means sermon preparation. It means organizing the rest of our time around sermon preparation, not vice versa. The strong inclination is to squeeze sermon preparation in around the edges. There is so much to do, so many meetings and people to see. My own life improved immensely when I acknowledged the fact that sermon preparation was my most important responsibility and deserved prime time. So that is what I give it.

Plan ahead. I've learned that sermons are like Scotch whiskey. The longer the time in the barrel, the better the product will be. Likewise, the shorter the preparation time, the more difficult the process will be, and I will find myself at my desk staring at an empty legal pad, praying for God to rescue me. So three times a year, once in the summer, once after Christmas, and once after Easter, I find a few days to plan ahead. I sit down with the Bible, lectionary, and a legal pad. I copy and read the texts for each Sunday and write a summary sentence for each. I want to get the whole sweep of what the lectionary wants me and the whole church to be thinking about. As a Presbyterian I have freedom to ignore the lectionary and go my own way, but I want to know what the whole church is dealing with weekly.

When that task is finished, for the next four months or so I write down the readings for each Sunday, on a single sheet, along with my thoughts, and already themes are emerging. That act, creating a page for each Sunday, is like opening a file. Stuff starts dripping in: newspaper articles, movies, concerts, stories. As they come, I clip or write them in the page. Usually there will be more material than I can use for the sermon.

Organize the week. Weekly preparation deserves prime time. Monday morning is for basic textual study and exegesis. I return to it early Tuesday morning. I spend Wednesday morning tracking down the resources I've been collecting. By late morning I have maybe twenty pages of notes. Before bed on Wednesday, I reread and redline all of it and reduce it to twenty or so simple sentences. That's when I stop, and on a good week I'm convinced the sermon starts to write itself while I'm sleeping. Thursday morning I lift from those twenty sentences the key ideas, and I start writing and don't stop until the sermon is done. I write it out longhand. I can do it without notes, but I know that I choose words better and create better sentences with a pen in my hand.

This is a major time investment that dictates the rest of the week. It is the task to which my people have called me. They are paying me, in Fred Craddock's wonderful description, to go to my study, close the door, wrestle with Scripture, and then report what I have discovered on Sunday morning.

A system like this also liberates the preacher from the worst possible circumstance—waiting until Saturday, or worse yet, Saturday night. I've done it a few times and hated it. So did my wife.

Pay attention to your relationships. Organizing life around the most important task means freeing up Saturday for family, errands, ball games, and picnics. Saturday night is for drinks, dinner, a movie, or concert, not sermon writing.

It is so easy to be consumed by this work that there is little time left for the most precious gift of all—people to love and care for. The work is never done. So it is imperative to learn how to say no. Pay attention to spouses, children, and dear ones.

My wife taught me early on the importance of boundaries by simply refusing to be a minister's wife, conforming to everyone's expectations. Together we decided that our children would not be PKs (preacher's kids). They would be our children. After years of missing one-time events in their lives because of church meetings, I simply stopped. "I'll have to leave the meeting early," I learned to say. "My son is playing basketball."

Be intentional about pastoral care. We are pastors. We will be preachers to the extent that we are pastors, accessible and available to our people. Our people will listen to us, allow us to be prophetic, to the extent that they know we care about them, love them, and will be there for them when they need us. Like sermon preparation, pastoral care requires intentionality and careful planning. It is also a ministry of the whole church, and so part of our task is to structure ways for it to happen, then train and empower people to be pastors. Care teams, organized to be present with and help people in crisis can, like Stephen Ministers, help the church with its ministry of caring.

Practice self-care. If you plan your sermons well, take care of yourself, and learn about boundaries and how to say no, you will have time for yourself. It is absolutely imperative to take care of spirit, intellect, and body. A concert, a play, a ballet, a baseball game, a movie, or an evening with a novel are integral to our health and happiness.

We are whole persons, and it is important for us ministers to practice the "holism" we preach. Regular exercise, walking, jogging, and swimming keep body and spirit refreshed, fit, and healthy.

Pray. Quiet moments at the beginning of the day, a psalm, devotional reading, an experience of openness and stillness in the presence of God have become a source of life to me. One of the lovely traditions at the church I serve is daily prayer for the staff and whoever else wishes to attend, a fifteen-minute service of Scripture and prayer for the world, the church, and for a dozen of our members, by name. We write letters to inform them that they will be prayed for, and we invite them to tell us anything they wish us to be mindful of as we pray for them. As I sign each of those letters, I think about them and their joys and concerns, their worries and challenges. I find myself experiencing the unity of the body of Christ and also the great privilege of being their pastor. As I approach retirement, I find myself loving ministry with a new clarity and affection, and I wish and pray that for all of us. There is, after all, so much to love.

Notes

1. Barbara Brown Taylor, *Leaving Church* (San Francisco: HarperSanFrancisco, 2006).
2. Frederick Buechner, *Secrets in the Dark: A Life in Sermons* (San Francisco: HarperSanFrancisco, 2006), 153.
3. Eileen Lindner, *Thus Far on the Way: Toward a Theology of Child Advocacy* (Louisville, KY: Witherspoon Press, 2006), 15.
4. Taylor, *Leaving Church*, 31.

6

Side Thoughts on Preaching for Those Who Must Stammer God's Unnamed Name

DAVID G. BUTTRICK

Generally, I avoid giving advice. Those of us who trip cheerily from blunder to blunder are seldom reliable when it comes to advice. Besides, advice giving can easily drift into irritating moralism. But the subject is preaching and the need is large, so perhaps a blunder may be better than nothing.

First, *stand in your pulpit scared*. No glib self-confidence for you. After all, your position is precarious. You are speaking for God in the presence of God. Now, unpack the previous sentence: (1) You do speak for God, and your words may well represent God in the minds of listeners. Moreover, you promote God's liberating purposes with your preaching. If you want a guide to God's purposes, spin the prohibitions of the Decalogue into positive statements. Or read the Beatitudes: The poor will be raised up, the hungry fed, the powerless empowered, peacemakers endorsed, and those who weep for the ways of the world mightily cheered. Add to those specifics a vision of cheerful human exchange: We are to serve one another with arms outstretched like waiters at table, and, without fear, we are to welcome others who serve us. God seems to want a serving society. So, yes, please remember you speak for God. But (2) realize all your speaking takes place in the Presence. God is a mysterious Consciousness, conscious of us. So stand in your pulpit scared. Yes, God is Mercy, and we are justified by God's

grace alone. But we should not presume on grace. Thus, for preachers, awe is the beginning of wisdom. Work hard so your words may be
fit for God's use. And say your prayers; asking God to help you set yourself aside—always a good idea. Speak for the sake of your people, for
they are a congregation God has given to your care. Ultimately, neighbor love undergirds preaching, and your immediate neighbors are in
pews listening to you.

Second, *do not suppose that all you need is a limp Bible and a heart
full of Jesus*. No, you need theology. Remember theology?—the course
you tried to doze through during your ministerial training. Even
before you open a page of the Bible you need theology. Without theology, these days people are reading Scripture from social or political
commitments—female/male, black/white, poor/rich, conservative/
liberal. Theology can help us to read Scripture from a faith larger than
social location, race, sex, or a voting record. But theology shapes
homiletic practice as well. In preaching, the metaphors you choose,
the examples you use, the ways in which you develop ideas, all are
guided by theological considerations. Homiletics is nothing more
than rhetoric under the tutelage of theology. In sum, good preachers
are always good theologians. Bad preachers are still dozing through
the theological books they always meant to read.

Third, *hold hands with the dying on a regular basis*. If you would
preach, keep in touch with the living and the dying. Be a faithful pastor. You need to cover some nearby hospital about every third day at
the least, listening and blessing in God's name. You can also drop by a
hospital on days when no other clergy may be there—Thanksgiving,
Christmas Day, New Year's Eve, the "glorious Fourth," days when an
emergency room can be busy. You might want to hang around and be
useful. When the phone rings in the night, go. People need you. After
someone's spouse has died you'll want to call every few days, then
every week, and then taper off, but don't forget the day. What do you
do in your show-up and stand-by ministry? Often nothing, but be
there, even if you feel awkward and useless. Don't catch yourself saying the same God-phrases in the same situations; people aren't situations to be treated with reused words. Above all, don't be silly and
suppose you are a parish executive somehow above human tears. Who
(in hell) wants to devote a life to institutional maintenance! Remember, churches don't save, God does. And ridiculous though it may

seem, you are God's picked-out pastoral representative. So you'll celebrate births, and preside at marriages with delight, and yes, hold hands with the dying, watching their labored breathing that will suddenly simply stop. The mystery of being born, of glad sexuality, and of dying goes along with preaching God's good news. Good preachers are on-the-job pastors and, because they internalize the laughter and the tears, they shape their words with tenderness. Oh, by the way, never take a dime for pastoral services—baptisms, marriages, funerals. Cash transactions corrupt pastoral ministry and thus can injure preaching.

Fourth, *be concerned for craft*. Not art, but craft. There have been books on "the art of preaching." Skip them. Preaching is a craft to be learned like carpentry or cooking. Ego-driven self-expression is not what's wanted. We can live without polished sermons, the kind that draw admiration from listeners. A good sermon moves in the minds of listeners like their own thoughts. They are not aware of your sermon as separate from their hearing. They certainly don't give a hoot for aesthetic considerations; neither should you. Instead, you will study homiletic craft. Preaching is not a one-to-one personal conversation. No, you are addressing a gathered congregation, which is an entirely different mode of speaking. In one-to-one conversation among friends you can discuss a number of subjects in a matter of minutes. But public speaking is a slowed-down system, carefully designed so ideas form naturally in the minds of your listeners. They don't merely hear; they must see and feel ideas. Meanings must be built in as permanent experience, something they will be able to recall as needed. Evidence indicates that it takes about three minutes to form each unit of meaning in the minds of your listeners. Simple two or three sentences won't accomplish much. So you will want to study homiletics.[1] And go to hear grand speakers whenever you can, then try to find out what does and doesn't work. Ideally preaching should be learned in apprenticeship.

Fifth, *you don't need to discuss yourself in sermons*. But some preachers do. They begin every sermon with themselves, with some reference to their personal experience over the past week. The result is that they split their focus between themselves and their subject matter. Who have they left out? Their congregation. Why do preachers need to talk about themselves? Do they crave affirmation? Or do they (mistakenly) believe that personal openness will improve their relatedness?

In my book *Homiletic*, I made up an example.[2] It went something like the following: *The other day driving around, I caught sight of a little girl in her front yard dancing in a sunbeam. I pulled over to watch, but she caught sight of me and stopped dancing. I felt like I'd killed something. Has anything like that ever happened to you?*

First, no one in the audience will associate my experience with anything in their own lives. Second, the audience will always attach my experience to me. (Will listeners suppose the preacher is a dirty old man who peeks at little girls?) When you tell stories of yourself, the two reactions will always follow; people will not associate your story with their own experience, and the example will always illustrate the speaker and nothing more. So what can you do? If the example is important, you can make it happen in minds of your listeners: *Have you ever watched children at play? Maybe a little girl in her front yard dancing in a sunbeam. But then, suddenly, she sees you watching and stops dancing, Don't you feel like you've ruined something beautiful?*

More often than not, a personal experience can be shifted into the consciousness of your congregation and suddenly become not only useful but powerful. If your experience is so unusual that it can't be designed to happen in the minds of listeners, it's too bizarre for preaching. But what about personal testimony? If employed often, it becomes fearfully redundant. If you must tell your congregation about your faith, you can get away with it about once every year. The congregation's faith is all-important, not yours. Remember the fixed rule: Preaching is all about neighbor love, and neighbor love means setting yourself aside.

Sixth, *though your preaching can be biblical, don't quote a lot of Scripture.* Some preachers try to weave biblical language throughout their sermons. Do they suppose that words from the Bible have magic properties? No, though words come from the Bible, they are ink-on-a-page, human words. The problem has to do with written-down biblical words being inserted in the midst of a speaker's language. Your own way of speaking is distinctive. If you insert another language, particularly from written texts, your listeners will have to adjust, and in the process of adjusting will no doubt lose the quote anyway. Biblical quotes scattered throughout a sermon will not produce meaning. A sermon may "smell" biblical in a rather general way, but your presenting of the gospel message may be disrupted. So study your Bible, and search deep biblical meanings, but don't clutter sermons with much quoting, even from Scripture.

Seventh, *don't be afraid of the prophetic.* Some preachers are prophetic on the basis of God's law. We can look backward: in covenant faithfulness, God has given us the redemptive guidance of commandments at Mount Sinai. God has gone along with us; we should be going along with God. But how much easier it is to be prophetic while looking toward God's future? All you have to do is to read through the Beatitudes to see what God has in mind. So if God wants peace on earth and goodwill exchanged within God's human family, then can we not speak out against a war in Iraq that has brought death to more than 700,000 Iraqis and displaced more than two million families from home and homeland, a war that has earned our nation's condemnation? Still more, the war has led to a collapse of our morality, with the use of torture being exhibit one. Why were most pulpits silent? Perhaps because most us were afraid to speak. We did not want to risk upsetting our largely conservative congregations. The future of God is the basis of prophetic speech. We speak while gazing at images of "kingdom" that Jesus hands out. Fear may call for homiletic smarts, but fear is not a good gift to offer God. Remember, you speak in the presence of God, so go deal with God, a God who speaks prophetic words to you.

Eighth, *help your people to bump into the mystery of God.* We are not merely acknowledging our limited "cloud of unknowing," but insisting that God's holiness is mysterious and quite alien to usual, human experience. So, for heaven's sake, don't try to fill your sermons with explanation, waving away the strangeness of God. No one has direct knowledge of God. And no one has an immediate experience of God. What we can know is our awed unknowing as we stand before the huge, holy mystery of God. Actually, we can't know one another; there is always a hidden dimension of self in other human beings, even well-married others. So, similarly, the full nature of God is quite beyond our knowing. But we can bow before the inexplicable Mystery.

Ninth, *for heaven's sake don't enumerate ideas in a sermon.* I have just done so, and it is an annoying practice. Saint Augustine recommended enumeration, but he was wrong. If listeners fix on the number that ticks off the start of a sentence, they will frequently fail to hear the idea that follows in the rest of the sentence. Enough! No more numbers and no more advice either. So there!

But, hold on, here's number ten: *everything is grace*. By all means, trust grace.

Notes

1. If I were picking an introductory homiletic text, I would certainly assign Thomas G. Long, *The Witness of Preaching*, 2nd ed. (Louisville, KY: Westminster John Knox Press, 2005).
2. David Buttrick, *Homiletic: Moves and Structures* (Philadelphia: Fortress Press, 1987).

7

Preaching in a Church Where the Culture Needs to Change

WILLIAM J. CARL III

S ince this is a book of advice for pastors as well as preachers, this chapter addresses a subject of pastoral leadership that I believe is crucial for the church these days. It's a crisis of leadership that directly affects how people hear sermons—the culture of conflict that leads to a strained civility in many congregations.

What difference does the culture make for preaching? It makes all the difference in the world. If the culture of the congregation you serve or are considering serving is dysfunctional, it doesn't really matter how much time you spend on creative exegesis, hermeneutical analysis, theological reflection, nifty outlines that move in and out of the text, scintillating illustrative material, or sentences that crackle. People are still going to be at each other's throats after they sing the last hymn and hear the benediction. You may think you are changing the culture with your sermons, and perhaps you're making a dent in it, but it will take more than the pulpit to create a new congregational culture. For this reason alone, I often tell pastors who are considering a move to another church to tell pastoral search committees, "We preachers have to give trial sermons; you congregations ought to have trial worship services. I'd like to come to your church on a Sunday as a visitor and see how I'm treated without anyone knowing that I am the candidate you are calling." In denominations such as the United Methodist Church, this wouldn't work, since pastors are generally appointed to their parishes. But even in those cases, it's still important to check out what the culture is like in the church you are entering.

If you are beginning a new ministry in a church that is divided, you are going to have some serious work to do as a pastoral leader, and preaching will only be part of it. If you have inherited a "preacher-killer" church (God forbid), watch your backside and find people you can trust who will let you know what the chatter on the street is so you can avoid being blindsided.

Imagine that you have started a new call in a church that has had its ups and downs but is fairly healthy and mature, and yet trouble still bubbles up when you least expect it. The truth is, no matter how perfect a particular parish may appear, there's bound to be conflict lurking somewhere just below the surface, even as there is in marriages that seem perfect to the outside world. There's no way to avoid conflict. The quotation really ought to read, "Wherever there are two or three gathered in the name of Christ, there's bound to be an argument!"

The point I want to make is not that we should try to avoid conflict altogether, which would be impossible, but that we should deal with it in a healthy and responsible manner. As I have said many times in parishes I have served, at Pittsburgh Seminary where I am president, and in national church meetings, "Real friendship in Christ means we have the right to disagree knowing that mutual affection and respect are not at stake."

I believe that the problem of unhealthy conflict is so serious in the twenty-first-century church that it's splitting denominations and congregations everywhere. Because of that, years ago I developed a program for building healthy, institutional cultures called "the Four S's" and have initiated it wherever I have worked, consulted, or lectured.

The Four S's are *(No) Secrets, (No) Surprises, (No) Subversion* and *(Lots of) Support*. I want you to understand each of these rules for healthy conflict and begin to live them, model them, and teach them to your church leaders and your congregation. If you do, you can actually change the culture of your parish—not overnight, of course, since real, substantive culture change takes years, so remember to be patient. If enough church leaders, both clergy and lay, would adopt these Four S's, we could, with God's help, change the culture of Christianity not only in America but around the world. When you change the culture in your church, you can preach the gospel at a deeper, more profound level than you have ever done before because people are less ego-driven, less divided, and ready to hear the gospel anew, and thus ready to share it with the world.

No Secrets

The goal here is to get people talking *to* each other and not *about* each other. Gossip and rumors can destroy a congregation, or any institution for that matter. The worst is when people speak negatively about others in e-mail, which is really stupid since anyone can eventually read what they write. My goal as a pastoral leader is to get individuals to go in person when they have a problem with someone else. Go not to attack but to let the other person know that something he or she said has caused dismay. Go in person, because it's always better for Christians to deal with conflicts face to face rather than behind each others' backs (read Matt. 5:21–26 for advice on how to do this). We don't need James to tell us, "Do not speak evil against one another, brothers and sisters" (Jas. 4:11). We know it's wrong intuitively. So gossip is out. Straight talk in person is in.

How do you get people to live the "No Secrets" rule? You can preach a series of sermons on it, but better yet, you can insist on it in new member classes, in orientation for new staff members, new elders, new deacons and other church leaders, and in the way your staff relates to each other and the parishioners. Most importantly, *you have to model it yourself*. You can't go around talking negatively about other pastors, educators, church leaders, or parishioners behind their backs or in a group. It's so easy to slip into it if you're not careful. Once you've laid this down as the kind of thing Jesus lived and taught, you need to call people on it in a gentle way when they break this rule, not like *Seinfeld*'s Soup Nazi—"No grace for you! You broke the 'No Secrets' rule!"—but as a shepherd who loves his or her sheep and wants the best for them. Otherwise, the gossip will continue even behind your back.

Does this mean that you never have anything confidential? Of course not. What it really means for us as pastoral leaders is *transparency*. You don't want people guessing where you're going or what you're thinking. Let them know. At the beginning of my first faculty meeting at Pittsburgh Seminary I said, "I've already heard fifteen things that Dr. Carl is going to do. Guess what? All of them are wrong. Next time you hear a rumor, I'd like for you to do two things: first, don't pass it on, and second, come to my office and I'll tell you if it's true or not." The board, faculty, administration, and staff don't have to guess what I'm thinking. It's all out there. And this simple rule alone has changed the culture. So the first rule of a community that practices "healthy conflict" is "No Secrets."

No Surprises

Here's another one that can nearly destroy all sorts of institutions but especially churches. How many times have you walked into a church board meeting or committee meeting and heard someone say, "I move that the education committee do so and so," and the person making the motion has never spoken to the chair of the education committee. It may be a good idea, but the chair of the education committee or the staff person resourcing that part of the church's ministry is now on the defensive because no one gave him or her a heads-up on what was coming. People who are surprised in this way may not say anything at the moment, but just beneath the surface they are seething. Then they either try to blunt the progress on what may be a very good idea, with arms-crossed, scowl-faced, passive-aggressive behavior, or they try to sink it behind the scenes by never once speaking to the person who made the motion in the first place. Either way, there is now tension in your church board or your pastoral or program staff that you didn't start yourself, a brush fire you have to put out before it gets too big.

Church leaders who surprise others are usually people who like to pull power plays and show they are in charge. Sometimes they do it inadvertently because they are rushed for time. Whatever the reason, the one who was blindsided is no doubt mad and frustrated and not feeling much like listening to your sermon on Christian love the next Sunday because he or she is now hearing it through the filter of an angry and aggrieved party. People who get surprised too often eventually decide they won't serve anymore and sometimes stop coming to church altogether, eventually drifting away—all because someone surprised them in a meeting one night! Imagine how much better the culture in your church would be if there were no surprises.

No Subversion

This one may be even worse than the first two. Let's say your church board or church committee had a very tense debate on a hot, somewhat controversial topic, and when the vote was taken you were in the minority. You're not very happy about the way things turned out because you feel strongly that this is the wrong way for your church to go. You know that you have avenues for appeal, such as motions to rescind and motions to reconsider, but you don't try either of these. You know that you are supposed to support the majority vote. Instead, you poison it in the parking lot. Subversion is one of the most insidious things happening in congregations these days. I've seen subversion destroy whole churches and institutions. You had an opportunity to speak your opposition to what you thought was a really dumb and misguided idea. And because you followed the "No Secrets" rule, you had your say, but you still lost the vote. But now, just as quickly forgetting the "No Secrets" rule, you go right out and gossip in a negative way about what your church board just passed after due deliberation.

Every pastoral leader has experienced parishioners who have done this. How do you prevent this? By preaching about it? That might help. But insisting on "No Subversion" with every leader in your parish during officer and new staff orientation and then modeling it yourself is usually even more effective. This is one I broke myself a couple of years after instituting the Four S's in a church I was serving. I didn't get as far as the parking lot. I was so mad about the way the vote had gone that night that I started in on it with some of the elders in the hallway right outside our meeting room as soon as the meeting was over. A couple of days later three elders invited me to lunch at a very nice restaurant. I didn't even see it coming. After a few pleasantries, one of them leaned forward and said, "Now, Bill, tell us again about the Four S's." I never broke any of them again after that!

Lots of Support

This is the cheerleading one, the kind Paul offered in his letter to the Philippians. We all need affirmation. We need to build up the body of Christ in true, agape love. Certainly there will be times when we have to "speak the truth in love," but for me the emphasis in that phrase is on speaking the truth *in love*. The older I get the more I realize that everyone in our families, on our church staffs, on our church boards, and in our congregations needs encouragement and positive reinforcement.

It should be clear by now that the Four S's represent both Old Testament ethics and wisdom, and New Testament community as envisioned by Jesus. The Decalogue and the Prophets pull no punches in speaking specifically about and directly to world and culture. Jesus, Paul, and the other New Testament writers hold nothing back in describing the way we are supposed to treat each other in this new community where, though active in the world, our citizenship is in heaven. Review especially Romans 12 to see the conduct expected in the new ecclesiology—no secrets, surprises, or subversion, but lots of support.

Imagine what it would be like to preach in a church with a positive, happy, and healthy culture. You can do that. It's not too late if you start today. You can create this sort of culture with God's help by insisting on it in your boards and by modeling it in your pastoral leadership. No Secrets, No Surprises, No Subversion, and Lots of Support—if all of us did it, we could change the church and thereby the world. I can guarantee one thing for sure: preaching is a lot more fun and definitely more rewarding in a culture like that.

8

Finding the Power to Preach When You're Exhausted

JANA CHILDERS

Whether you are a new preacher or one who has been around the homiletical barn a couple of times, you get tired. Most preachers get not only tired but worried. Many preachers are not only worried but anxious about their craft. We picture the good folks who come up the steps on a Sunday morning looking for a glimpse of "the glorious church without spot or wrinkle" and we wonder about our ability to produce.

Sometimes the advice we receive hurts more than it helps us with this worry. Some of us, for example, were told by our well-meaning mentors to spend an hour in the study for every minute in the pulpit. For many of us that turned out to be a more reliable producer of depression than inspiration. Our failure to log seventeen or thirteen or even eight hours haunted us. We added the guilt to the rest of our silent load and trudged on—tired.

Through preaching's long history there is no doubt that the Holy Spirit has used the sermons of tired preachers to great effect. There is no doubt that Jesus, Paul, John Chrysostom, Aimee Semple McPherson, and Billy Graham preached while tired. There is no doubt that you will preach while tired many times in what is, let us hope, the long haul of your ministry. But there is also no doubt that preaching while tired is not the way preaching is meant to work.

There is something in good preaching that is all about energy. It crackles and zips and constricts the throat. There is something that rises up and spreads out with a life all its own. There is something that lifts or pokes or sucks a person in. And whatever that something is, it is not a mere ornament of good preaching but an essential ingredient of the thing. It is part of what makes preaching "preaching" and not "public speaking." It is part of what is unique about preaching. It is something that seems to happen without our help and in spite of our tiredness.

Where does this peculiar energy come from? The advice I most welcome as a preacher and most often give as a teacher is about tracking down the source. I know this power in my own preaching process and see it in the preachers I work with in at least three arenas: power in the body, in the word, and in the spirit.

Power in the Body

The truth will out. "A man cannot lie. If he lies with his lips he will chatter the truth from his fingertips." This is rough translation of something Freud said in *The First Dream*, published in 1905. (Since Freud is the one speaking it seems appropriate to leave the sexist language in.) It's a powerful expression of an important truth that, a century after Freud first said it, affects the ministry of both men and women. The truth will out, and it will be the truth about you—about how you feel about yourself, about being there, about your sermon, about the people you are looking out at. The reason it is powerful is because the unconscious is powerful, both in the preacher and for the listener. My first two pieces of advice are about great ways to tap this power:

Mind your feet. Speech teachers have said for centuries, perhaps millennia, that the most honest members of the body are the feet. Have you ever wondered why futzy feet are so common in new preachers? You know what I mean. Feet that make small, unintentional movements. Futzy feet are feet that never seem to keep still, that distract from or work against the message coming out of the preacher's mouth. They're nervous feet whose movement serves only one purpose—and that a selfish one—namely, to dissipate the preacher's anxious energy. They are common in new preachers because they are the result of ambivalence. Futzy feet express a divided mind—a preacher torn between fight and flight—between staying to preach and beating a path for the door.

Harnessing the nervous energy of the feet is not only a good idea for the moments we spend preaching in (or especially out of) the pulpit but is a great place to start the creative process. In the study, pacing can free and focus creative energy. It is not accidental that many of the most effective African American preachers of our day compose their sermons while pacing, addressing first the wall, then the closet door, then the tree branch on the other side of the window. Do you want your sermon to have life, a sense of movement? Start with your feet. Discipline and harness the energy that resides there. It can fund your creativity and add polish to the preaching moment.

Know yourself. Long before Myers-Briggs offered us its very useful personality types, speech teachers and theatre directors were sizing up the performance style of their students. Each performer will fall into one of three groups. He or she will be dominantly head-oriented, heart-oriented, or gut-oriented. Although each of us has the ability to express all three traits when they are called for, we tend naturally to one more than the others. Each type has its own "home base" or nonverbal style.

People who are dominantly head-oriented favor a cluster of nonverbal behaviors that use the fingertips and eyes. Think of the engineers in your congregation, or picture your favorite Old Testament professor. Head-oriented people steeple their fingers, point, put a finger next to the mouth and squint more than other people. You can see the thinking process take place in their eyes. They are parsers, analyzers, discerners, dividers, and their favorite gestures show them doing those things.

Heart-oriented people favor the palms and cheeks when it comes to nonverbal expression. Like gospel singers and Pentecostal worshipers, they express their emotions with extended palms and active cheeks.

The nonverbal communication of gut-oriented people is focused in the torso. The chest, the upper arms, the back of the arm—these are their key expressers. The sports fan's gesture that starts with a raised, bent arm and a fist and brings the elbow straight down very quickly with a "Yes!" is the quintessential gesture of a gut-oriented person.

Knowing whether you are dominantly head-oriented, heart-oriented, or gut-oriented will keep you from trying to bend Romans 8 (a dominantly head-oriented passage) into a sportscast, or Daniel 5 (Belshazzar's feast, a dominantly gut-oriented text) into a philosophical lecture. Learning to work with the particular energy of a text not only saves you from kicking against the pricks; it frees the best kind of energy—the kind that is natural to the text and to you.

Power in the Word

The next two pieces of advice are based on my understanding of the relationship between Scripture and preaching. Some of contemporary preaching's grayness is surely attributable to the way preachers underuse texts. Some of us springboard from juicy, detailed, technicolor texts into safe, little, pastel sermons. We shouldn't be surprised when these sermons turn out to be what one of my colleagues describes as the kind that "just dribble down the front of the pulpit and out into the aisles."

Be specific. Interpret the text with as much specificity as you can. It may be that we don't know enough about the biblical writers to crack their codes or even to ascertain whether or not they had them. Luke, for example, is a great Gospel that contains indispensable elements of the biblical story. It's difficult to imagine Christianity without Luke. But the question of whether there is an overarching strategy that organizes Luke's Gospel is a real one. Mark, though, is a completely different matter. Mark is crafted to advance an agenda. Mark is strategic. Passages are placed by design. The use of key words and themes is orchestrated. Identifying these makes it possible for the preacher to be less global and much more specific with the hermeneutical leaps. Mark is pushing a particular point of view. You and I don't have to agree on what it is. Theories abound. Grab on to one and try it. See what difference it would make to the bottom line or the application section of your sermon. See if you can refine it. Preach at least occasionally a sermon that resists seeing the text as a treasure trove for timeless truths and takes Mark on his own terms.

Be textual. Preach a sermon that truly deserves to be called a "textual sermon." Let the question that prompts the sermon as well as the answer the sermon offers arise from the text. Don't stop at preaching sermons on the "love of God" or "love of neighbor." There are lots of texts in the Bible that can be preached that way. But it is important for a preacher to wrestle with the ones that say that and more. Occasionally preach a sermon that treats these texts. Many preachers seem to outgrow their seminary years soon after they start receiving a paycheck. We use the skills we learned in school less and rely on our own spiritual gizzard more. Occasionally preach a sermon that makes good use of your formal education.

Power of the Spirit

This last piece of advice belongs to the province of the Holy Spirit. It is beyond foolhardy, of course, to try to generalize about the movement of the Spirit. God has God's own way of working with preachers, and a good deal of it knocks us off our chairs. Some of us can think of times when we have been blown into the next zip code. But perhaps for the purposes of this section we can merely observe that the Holy Spirit often seems to work in the realm of human emotion.

Make your peace with emotion. Nobody wants to look like the tear-streaked televangelist who prowls the edge of the stage with nose dripping and glasses fogging. Most of us give that kind of emotion a wide berth, and for good reason. Emotions are a powerful force for good or ill. But honest emotions, disciplined emotions, emotions that can in any sense be said to be under the control of or consecrated to the use of the Holy Spirit have a legitimate role to play in all kinds of preaching. Indeed, it is hard to imagine powerful preaching apart from them.

Emotions elaborate thoughts. They arise from within us and attach themselves to words, adding layers of meaning. Most of us know the experience: Your mind is thinking the word, your mouth is preparing to form it, your mental motion picture screen is conjuring up the image, and all of a sudden up from your toes come the tears or the laugh or the choke. Emotions elaborate, they flesh out the bone of a word, they connect the electrical circuits within us and between us and the listeners, and they help do what Charles Bartow describes as "turning ink into blood."

Power Source

On one level, the last thing a tired preacher needs is advice. If any of the above makes you feel heavy or guilty or tenser than you were when you started reading, I hope you will disregard it. To the extent that any of the above points you toward the energy God makes available to us in preaching, I'm glad for it. In either case, though, what is important is the attention you give to the task of finding out what about the preaching task buzzes or frees or lifts you—and to the Source of that energy on whose graciousness all depends.

9

The Signature Sermon

FRED B. CRADDOCK

Those who not only preach but who also try to keep abreast of conversations in the discipline have surely observed how such conversations proceed. One feature or component of preaching will be thoroughly and almost endlessly discussed in books and seminars. Finally, someone will remark that other aspects of preaching, no less important, are being neglected. For example, prolonged accent on *how* to preach eventually comes under the judgment of silence about *what* to preach. Or vice versa. Or only so many seminars can be held on the person in the pulpit as a factor in preaching until someone asks, "But what about the persons in the pew?" Or vice versa. Good point, but what can be done about it?

No self-respecting preacher or teacher of preaching really intends to create such an imbalance in conversations about preaching, but it seems to be built into the nature of fruitful discussion. Being careful to give everything equal time at the same time is deadly dull and sterile. To say everything is to say nothing. The alternatives seem to be either total silence or focusing on one thing and acknowledging necessary but temporary neglect of other topics. If you use a marker to underline key sentences when reading a textbook and discover at the end of a page that every line has been underscored, what have you achieved?

Even so, some who stand in the pulpit and bear the burden of the sermon have the feeling that some of us who write and lecture on preaching get on "kicks" and then treat our "kicks" messianically. "Can we not be given guidance on both the What and the How of preaching, on both the preacher and the listener, on both the tradition of the historic faith and personal experience of the gospel? You who lecture on such matters may have the luxury of choosing one or the other, but we who preach every week deal with all of it every week." This observation carries within it enough truth and enough pain that the following paragraphs are offered as an attempt to respond.

I recommend that every preacher prepare and deliver what may be called a "Signature Sermon." We are familiar with the designation "signature" in our culture: a chef has a signature dish, a singer a signature song, an instrumentalist a signature style, an artist a signature color or angle of vision. For example, a glow of golden light on an object or a room or a face was Rembrandt's "signature." A Signature Sermon would therefore be the preacher's own, clearly and unquestionably. Obviously it is not borrowed or plagiarized, but beyond being one's own, it is not so special that it does not resemble the main body of one's preaching. If the sermon is so unusual as to *appear* to be the work of another, it is not a Signature Sermon. The Signature Sermon will embody the preacher's accustomed ways of quoting Scripture, alluding to Scripture, echoing Scripture. It will include favorite literary references and often-stated moral and ethical accents. It will be fueled by the preacher's familiar points of passion. And the Signature Sermon will be relieved now and then by the preacher's own brand of humor. Briefly stated, this sermon will be so identified with the one who delivers it that the listeners will be able to say, "That is our preacher." Just as a careful student of Scripture can say, even when no reference is given, "That is Paul" or "That is Luke," so can the hearer or listener identify the author of the Signature Sermon.

But the Signature Sermon, personal in many ways, is not private; it is self-disclosing, but it is not about oneself. There is an important difference between holding the camera and being on camera. The Signature Sermon is one in which the listeners can also identify themselves. But it is not parochial; it does not so completely focus on one event, one time and place that it is not at all portable. No major substantive modifications would be necessary before it would have meaning for another congregation. This is not to say the sermon is generic, a one-size-fits-all speech for all occasions. It is not addressed "to whom it may concern," but this sermon does speak to and for the larger church. The congregation that hears it is heir to and witness to the received tradition of faith. The sermon passes along that tradition, not in a rubber-stamp way but with that self-criticism appropriate to any healthy tradition or institution. In this sense, the Signature Sermon is both recital and prophecy.

None of this means that the preacher is to abandon for this sermon the qualities of good composition and delivery that have served well in every sermon: imaginative language, conversation between characters in the sermon, appropriate analogies, persons as well as ideas, and movement with anticipation, to name only a few. In other words, the more important the What, the more important the How.

What, then, distinguishes the Signature Sermon? It gathers up in one message what the preacher believes, what the congregation believes, and what the historic church believes, framed in such a way as to remind, inform, correct, and call to a new level of discipleship. It will be a bit longer than other sermons that interpret a particular biblical text or topic and urge a particular response. Such sermons over time tend to notch every tree but taken together do not lead the parishioners through the forest. The Signature Sermon marks a path through the woods and makes clear this is who we are, whence we came, whither we go, and why we are here.

Just think what this does for the preacher! The preparation itself can be a delightfully demanding exercise in including, excluding, and arranging major units of the Christian faith story. There is none of that weekly "I have to get up a sermon" pressure. Rather, there is the elevating pressure of size: this is the biggest sermon one can preach. The preacher can assume the parishioners are interested because the sermon is important, and in the final analysis, what is truly interesting is that which is important and which touches life at its deepest need. Just think what the Signature Sermon does for the congregation! In a culture of disconnects and fragments, here is *the* story, the metanarrative within which the church can hear its name and find its place. In churches that have been struggling to survive on homiletical tidbits, be assured a Signature Sermon would be welcome. Be prepared for requests for copies. Some minds and hearts have over the years shrunk to the size of the pulpit menu, so they will want to read the sermon after hearing it. "Finally I know who we are and what church is." "I have been ashamed of my vague efforts to witness to my faith; now I have something to say." "This sermon goes into my memory bank, and I will draw on it again and again." Quotations from and allusions to the Signature Sermon will appear regularly in church school classes and fellowship conversations. Not that everyone agrees with everything in the sermon, but there is something of substance to discuss. Over time the sermon will become a part of the consciousness of the faith community.

How does one prepare a Signature Sermon? First, remember that the primary subject is God. The sermon announces who God is and what God is doing in the world. Second, choose a broad framework adequate to carry a large message. The possibilities for such a framework are many; only a few will be suggested here. One may use a chronological approach, moving from creation to new creation. Or one may employ a classic portrayal of God as Creator, Provider, Redeemer. Or if one belongs to a faith tradition that regularly recites the Apostles' Creed, then that faith statement could be unfolded in the Signature Sermon. The preacher may choose to make the sermon episodic, touching on the major events of the biblical narrative, perhaps held together by a refrain. A line from a familiar Scripture text or a repeated line from a favorite hymn might serve such a purpose. Recall the narrative in Hebrews 11: "By faith . . . ; By faith . . ."

Continuing suggestions for a sermonic framework, consider the rhetorical form called the farewell address. The farewell address allows for a full recital of past, present, and future. Examine again the farewell addresses of Joshua (Josh. 24), Moses (Deut. 33), Stephen (Acts 7), and Paul (Acts 20). Nonbiblical examples abound: General Washington's farewell to the troops, or General McArthur's farewell to the Congress of the United States. Please beware—it is not the "farewell" that commends these models. Any hint of "This may be my last sermon here" will be heard for what it is: emotional blackmail. This particular form commends itself because of the breadth of its recital.

Let two other suggestions suffice. One could prepare a Signature Sermon consisting entirely of passages of Scripture. For example, one could begin with Genesis 1:1 and conclude with either Revelation 21:1–5a or 22:16–17. In between, the preacher has the tough but refreshing task of choosing among the many voices that carry forward the story. (Citing the references in the sermon would be more disruptive than helpful.) Finally, the sermon could be structured biographically, letting the stories of principal biblical characters provide the components of the master narrative.

Needless to say, one fact remains regardless of the frame or pattern: the Signature Sermon will not easily or quickly be prepared. There will be many additions, deletions, and rearrangements, but the benefits of clarity that only focus can give, and the abundance of fresh discoveries that only exploring can give will more than compensate for the time and work. But keep in mind that the Signature Sermon will be preached again and again. Do not let the issue of stewardship of time be a question. One can hardly think of a wiser investment of time, study, and prayer. If there is any doubt in the preacher's mind, ask the listeners.

Once a rough draft emerges, lay it aside, get some distance. After a time, return to it, but now in an artistic rather than a research mode. Remember this is a sermon, prepared for the ear rather than the eye. How does it sound? Are the sentences lively? Does one move in the sermon anticipate the next? Does the listener have confidence the sermon is going somewhere, having in its movement a sense of an ending? Does the vocabulary appeal to sight, sound, touch, taste, or smell? Do the characters within the sermon act and speak, and are there genuine conversations within the sermon? After all, the Bible is primarily conversation: God said, Eve said, Noah said, Moses said, Rachel said, Mary said, Paul said, Jesus said. It is the conversational nature of the text that draws in the reader, and thus the absent becomes present and the reader (listener) becomes a partner in the process, contributing thought and feeling. When such a speaker-listener partnership is formed, the preacher is not tempted to dump prematurely conclusions and answers into the listener's ear.

Asking these and other such rhetorical questions of the rough draft transforms that draft into a sermon. It would be unwise to assume that because the Signature Sermon is more substantive, more grand in scale, more important than many pieces in one's homiletical repertoire, it will automatically gain and hold the attention of the congregation. On the contrary, because it is a Signature Sermon, there is all the more reason to bring to its content the best of one's rhetorical skills, and to its delivery, passion.

It is appropriate to preach the Signature Sermon once a year, and on the same Sunday of the year. One should choose a Sunday not already busy with other matters, such as raising the budget or promoting the children in church school. Why not Pentecost, All Saints' Day, or the anniversary of the founding of the congregation? The Sunday of the Signature Sermon should be treated as a high day, well advertised within and outside the congregation. Let all members, enquirers, and visitors know what is happening that day. After a few years of preaching the Signature Sermon, the church will not be saying, "Oh no, not again—been there and done that." Rather, there will be a growing sense of anticipation; attendance will grow rather than decline. And why? Because on this Sunday, unlike any others, the story of God will be shared most fully. Because dots will be connected. Because the listeners, clearly and without apology, will identify themselves as a community of faith and not simply as folk who happen to attend church services. And because of the unusual power of recognition. Having heard this sermon several times now, the listener will recognize and remember and own the message. "This," says the listener, "is what I would say if I were a preacher. And it is so important I have brought along a few friends."

10

Dealing with Diversity

MIGUEL A. DE LA TORRE

Recently, that great modern-day theologian, Steven Colbert of the popular Comedy Central show *The Colbert Report*, began accepting applications for the position of his very own "black friend." Realizing the importance of political correctness, Colbert thought it would be crucial to have a black friend he could point to in case he was ever accused of being a racist. He was so committed to the effort of not appearing to be racist that, before choosing from the pool of applicants, he had to ask someone else which ones were black because he was naturally, of course, "colorblind." Don't we all claim this? Unfortunately, Colbert's approach to racially and ethnically diversifying his cadre of friends is similar to the approach many churches take in trying to diversify their congregations. For some churches, the hope of diversification is more for the sake of political correctness than to create a new community.

Several years ago about thirty local white pastors gathered to discuss how best to diversify their congregations so as to be an example to the entire community. Tired of preaching to a sea of whiteness, they wanted to have their congregations conform more closely to the ideal church model illustrated in the book of Revelation, where those surrounding the throne of God represent "every tribe, language, people, and nation" (7:9–10). Although I appreciated their show of sincerity, I knew we were in trouble when I noticed that, including myself, there were only two ministers of color in the room. For about an hour the white pastors mainly congratulated each other for their foresight in dealing with issues of diversity within their congregations and towns. They went on to devise plans of action to achieve their noble goals: inviting a pastor of color to preach from each pulpit, forming a committee with a church of color in an attempt to bring the congregations together, or providing charity to a church of color in financial need. I found it interesting that no one bothered to ask the only two ministers of color in the room for their advice or concerns about some of the ideas being floated. Finally, after an hour of listening to strategies that I knew would never work, and worse, would give these pastors the excuse of saying that they tried but the communities of color were simply "not interested," I spoke up.

"Why," I asked, "do you assume I would even *want* to worship at your church? After centuries of exclusion, why should I come running now that you think it makes your church look good by having a black or brown face in the pew to prove that your congregations aren't racist?" My questions were not very well received. Nevertheless, I went on to say that it was difficult for me to pray while sitting next to the banker who will charge me an extra point of interest because my last name sounds Hispanic. It's hard to shout praises to the Lord while being stared at by the police officer who gave me a ticket for driving under the influence of being Hispanic. It's challenging to proclaim the mercies of my God knowing that sitting across the aisle is a parishioner who refuses to show mercy toward the undocumented. Unless those within the congregation begin to deal honestly and seriously with their white supremacy and class privilege, it is unlikely that I, and I suspect most believers of color, will pretend to forget what goes on *outside* the church building and just come on in.

Even if I did attempt to join such a church, I would find myself an exile within the congregation. While three-hundred-year-old Germanic hymns may stir the souls of Euroamericans, they do absolutely nothing spiritually for me. How can I praise the Lord in the language and style of a different culture? Where are my *coritos*? When do I get to hear the *testimonios* of my brothers and sisters? Worship for many of my people has less to do with presenting a timed schedule of activities and more of being a *fiesta*, a party in which everyone participates. And like most parties, it matters little if you go beyond the allotted time.

Even if members from marginalized churches are persuaded to join white churches, there are terrible consequences for churches situated in the hood or *barrio*. Political correctness for white congregations has a devastating effect for churches of color. As some within marginalized communities move toward middle-class status, they become a hot commodity for white churches to recruit. Having, in the words of Senator Biden, "articulate, bright, clean and a nice-looking" people of color join white congregations means that churches of color will suffer a brain-drain as well as a loss of middle-class tithes that are sorely needed to minister to those left behind. Diversification for white churches reinforces the struggle that churches of color face.

We are thus faced with the question, "What is the best advice that can be given to white ministers wishing to diversify their churches?" Or to answer Rodney King's immortal question, "Can't we all just get along?" No church should consider diversifying unless it first gets "saved." That is, the congregation as a whole must crucify its sins upon the cross of Jesus Christ. More specifically, the church members must nail their white supremacy and class privilege on the cross so that they can become new creatures in Christ. Becoming a new creature in Christ is not to be taken figuratively, but literally. The question that the church must ask itself is how much it is willing to change to become a new place where all can come to worship the Lord. The church wishing to diversify will never succeed while holding on to the attitude that "this is the way we've always done it and if you want to join us, you must convert and become like us." The church that is "saved" is less concerned with converting the world to its doctrine or way of worshiping God. Rather, it is focused on how much it must be converted to become more Christlike in order to be relevant to a hurting and disjointed world. Such a church follows the example laid out by that first Christian community recorded in the book of Acts. This early church converted from its prejudices in order to reach the world for Christ. Acts depicts how that first church had to accept Gentiles as fellow believers, renounce circumcision, and appoint women to lead churches in order to follow the movement of God's Spirit. As this early church encountered a multicultural world, it changed so that others could become followers of Christ without having to convert to some sociopolitical cultural norm. In essence, the book of Acts is the story of how God's Spirit subverts the self-imposed religious superiority of the church.

Besides radically challenging the co-option of Christianity by a Euroamerican culture, the church must also become a proactive transforming agent within the community. Will its members, and not just the pastor, stand in solidarity with the hungry, thirsty, naked, alien, sick, and imprisoned against the forces of institutionalized violence? Is the church willing to place everything on the line (including its investment portfolio) for the sake of the least of these? And here is the real question to answer: Is the church willing to actively dismantle the very institutionalized societal power structures designed to protect its white privilege and class preference?

Ministers desiring diversity will succeed if, instead of forming a committee to deal with the issue, they create a *familia*, a family where all come together to defend and uplift its members. Relationships of caring, as opposed simply to diversifying the congregation, become crucial in understanding the needs of churches of color. To stand in solidarity with the marginalized, to walk with the oppressed, to share the fate of the disenfranchised, and to fight for justice with the dispossessed, is costly. It can cost the church the trappings of respectability, it can even cost the minister her or his job; therefore, counting the cost of discipleship becomes crucial. The irrelevance of cultural Christianity is reversed through its radicalization. And there is nothing more radical than to stand with churches of color over against one's own self-interest, bringing to fruition the gospel call of placing the needs of the other before one's own.

But how does a minister lead his or her congregation toward such a vision of salvation? By preaching liberation—liberation from sin. All too often, sermons preached at white churches concentrate on personal piety—that is, how to be a better individual Christian, how to pray more, how to walk closer with Jesus, how to claim more joy, or how to trust God more. However, such sermons fail to connect with those who are suffering from racial or ethnic discrimination and injustices within the community. All too often the inward piety (a spiritual manifestation of a hyperindividualistic society) of those from the dominant culture outweighs Christ's call for us to practice social justice. The purpose of the churches' sermons and teachings is not to interpret proper individual piety but rather to change reality. Any sermon that fails to make the reality faced by the least among us the point of origin, or that is grounded on abstract discussions rather than actual praxis, may be Christian speculation, but it is certainly not what Christianity requires from its disciples.

When a white congregation's consciousness is raised to consider the plight of its neighbors of color, the hope of diversifying one's congregation becomes a reality. But even if the congregation fails to diversify, the church will hopefully have discovered its own salvation through its solidarity with the marginalized. One engages in the process of liberation not to achieve the ultimate goal of having more faces of color in the congregation. One engages in the process of liberation for the sole purpose of becoming the church of Jesus Christ, and leaving it up to God as to who joins the effort. The book of Acts describes the first Christians as "praising God and having the goodwill of all the people. And day by day the Lord added to their number those who were being saved" (2:47).

White churches need to be sensitive to how their push for diversity can negatively impact churches of color. For many churches of color, the poverty and marginalization they face within the community is reflected within their churches. As some members obtain middle-class status, or their children achieve higher education, they become the type of "diversity" white churches want. Recruiting such parishioners deprives their home churches of their resources and presence. If white churches are serious about diversity, then their best contribution to the cause may be to help strengthen churches of color rather than stealing their sheep. Standing in solidarity with such churches may require the privileged church to ask simply, "How do *you* want us to walk with you?" and thus forsake the illusion that the white church knows what is best.

For several centuries now, white supremacy has refused to allow all of God's children to sit together in a room for the purpose of singing praises to the Creator of all. Centuries of normalizing and legitimizing segregation simply cannot be washed away within a generation because those in power had an "Aha!" moment. Such a proposition would only continue the arrogance of those who confuse their power with the power of God. Maybe someday congregations will represent "every tribe, language, people, and nation." But to force the issue now, without doing the work of dismantling institutionalized segregation, would reduce diversity to tokenism. The seeds planted by white churches actively seeking justice today may in some future generation produce the fruit of diversity. The process promises to be long, difficult, and perilous. But we can begin to undo the consequences of centuries of the sin of white supremacy by replacing the present, prevalent separation of the people of God with the idea and reality of the *familia* of God in which one's skin color or ethnicity does not dictate who gathers in which building to praise the Lamb that sits upon the throne.

11

Being Repairers of the Breach

KATHARINE RHODES HENDERSON

As a daughter of a preacher and seminary professor, I vowed never to become one or marry one, and yet I have done both. After a profoundly invigorating atheistic period in late high school and early college, I became reconnected to my Christian faith after reading Hans Küng's *On Being a Christian*, and went to seminary with enormous curiosity and many questions. What I found was *the church* in the form of West Park Presbyterian, right in the heart of New York City's Upper West Side. It was a scrappy, run-down, physically depressing space, dysfunctional by any benchmarks of administrative excellence, but what happened inside was glorious. A small but genuinely racially and ethnically diverse congregation was completely committed to being involved in the neighborhood and the world: welcoming its neighbors from housing projects into the church; lobbying the New York City government for systemic change around housing for the poor; launching a national peacemaking ministry for nuclear disarmament; providing programs for the elderly poor and visiting them in their homes; and offering an after-school tutoring program for the unruly children and teenagers of the neighborhood who had nowhere else to go. It was messy, teeming humanity unlike anything I had ever experienced. There was no doubt that we were standing on holy ground. I felt I had found the kingdom of God, and with this experience came my own sure call to ministry.

I begin with the autobiographical, because returning in memory to one's original sense of call with its people, location, voices, sights, smells, and vocabulary is a touchstone for a lifetime of ministry. This primal experience of ministry at West Park Presbyterian was defining, because it reinforced for me the fundamental truth that the church does not exist for itself alone, or even primarily, but for the world. My advice to preachers and pastors is bookended by two texts, one from Isaiah 58 and the other from Jesus' postresurrection appearance to his disciples in the Gospel of John, where he cooks fish for them and reminds them of the central tenet of their mission: "Feed my sheep." The words from Isaiah vividly remind us that God calls us "to loose the bonds of injustice" in tangible form—"to free the oppressed, to break every yoke, to share bread with the hungry and bring the homeless poor into your house." The promise for such action is God's presence: "Then you shall call and the Lord will answer; you shall cry for help, and he will say, 'Here I am.'" Actions of justice, mercy, and peace will carry us into the role Isaiah prescribed for us: "repairers of the breach," "restorers of streets to live in."

The role I covet for pastors and preachers is that of public leader, activist, and servant. In many ways this is counterintuitive. It goes against the grain of the demands of congregations who prefer that their ministers stay close to home to care for their needs; it challenges the image of minister as corporate executive or competent manager; it reverses the current invisible status of religious leaders in the public square—a phenomenon documented by an Auburn Seminary research study called *Missing Connections*.[1] And, practically, where is there time in the busy schedule of any preacher and pastor for a public calling?

Yet I suggest that the biblical mandate for justice-seeking public leadership is undeniable, and further, that participation as a public leader keeps ministry fresh and alive as nothing else can. A colleague in ministry, also a leader in a national peace initiative, described this movement for me in the following way:

> I was a local pastor engaged on both local and far-reaching issues, but always with a sort of local parish perspective. I

never got so far into global things that I forgot the shut-ins' Communion. I was always able to stretch in both directions simultaneously, and those directions stimulated and energized each other.[2]

I suggest that this stretching, this bridging beyond the walls of the parish, is a core ingredient of faithfulness and also salutary—good for your health, that is, and for those with whom you minister who may go and do likewise as you lead the way. A publicly active role for religious leaders was certainly envisioned by John Calvin, who believed that the role of magistrate was a higher calling than that of minister.

Another colleague who practices this stretching, Sister Helen Prejean, a Catholic religious leader who has led a movement against the death penalty, goes so far as to call her public ministry an "essential spiritual dynamic," or I would suggest, a spiritual *discipline*:

> Visiting with people on Death Row, to me, is the anchor. That's the baseline. Being with murder victims' families and praying with them—that's the personal. And every person is a universe. My speaking comes out of those experiences, and I think that's why the speaking thing has been so good. . . . If I didn't maintain personal experiences with people, I would drift out of it, or I'd start putting gloves on and I'd be removed from it. You know, solidarity with poor people and being in their company, and being involved with people who are suffering is an *essential spiritual dynamic*. Without that you begin to drift away, and you begin to do these commentaries on your experiences—once removed, twice removed, three times removed. So, the presence of people suffering is just essential.[3]

So what does the spiritual discipline of public ministry look like practically, and how is it to be achieved and sustained? I suggest four strategies.

First, it involves allowing your heart to be moved by a particular pressing public issue. Where does your passion for justice live? Is it the environment and global warming, or the local incinerator whose presence precipitates asthma in neighborhood children? Is it immigration policy through the lens of an undocumented worker in your community whose deportation separates him from his wife and children? Is it the homeless who loiter, sleep, and urinate on the steps of the church, or a church member who loses her home and livelihood through a layoff and mortgage foreclosure?

When your heart is broken open, when the engine of empathy is activated, you must become literate, even expert about that issue. What systemic issues drive the injustice underlying this particular human situation? Who are the local, national, international players—the principalities and powers involved? What theological and biblical perspectives pertain? How can you and your flock make connections as activists around the issue? What difference can you make as people committed to healing and repairing the world? One of the most important recent movements that church people made in this regard was mobilizing in the aftermath of Hurricane Katrina. They made important initial strides to welcome the stranger and to help rebuild. The next steps would be to understand more deeply the racial and class divisions that played into that tragic scenario in the first place and to do the systemic analysis about the growing gap between "haves and have-nots."

Deep exploration and engagement with a public issue has an important by-product that offers particular hope for preachers. Sister Helen Prejean testifies that her intimate relationship with the public issue of the death penalty has made all the difference in her preaching and public speaking. Her words ring true!

This brings me to the second strategy: developing your own media savvy. Speaking out in public may require a different set of skills than those required for the pulpit. If we are to become visible and credible spokespersons on the public issues that break our hearts, we will need to do some cross-training to develop new oratory muscles. Through our work at Auburn Seminary we offer speaker training for religious professionals. I have seen some of the best preachers brought to their knees with anxiety in front of a TV camera. Yet to use radio and television, op-eds or blogs, we need to learn how to convey a theological message in a sound-bite world. If we have internalized the norm to keep silent in public about our religious faith—feeling that religion is fundamentally a private matter—or if we feel daunted by a public that is both diverse and secular, it may at first be difficult to find a language of meaning that translates into a broader public. Yet that is what we are called to do. It will bring you into contact with a younger generation and with those who are not religiously affiliated, both of which represent desired constituencies today where size matters, and where we're all trying to figure out how to pass along the faith.

This new role of public spokesperson will take you to tables of conversation in your community where ministers do not usually go—which is exactly the point: gatherings of businesspeople, politicians, and educators, meetings of the school board, in the town hall, at legislative hearings, in cultural gatherings. To be "players" in the world around you is the goal, not in order to capture headlines for yourself but rather to strategize with others to solve urgent human needs and to contribute your unique resources to the table.

The third strategy to become a more effective public leader is to explore the religiously pluralistic environment that awaits you outside your front door. The United States is the most religiously diverse country in the world, yet we as religious leaders often know little about other religious traditions. As Robert Wuthnow documents, we often play an avoidance game.[4] Our seminaries are only now beginning to prepare students for a pluralistic world, yet religious diversity is one of the most exciting challenges and opportunities facing pastors today.

As religious leaders who want to be repairers of the breach, we can begin to heal the divides between and among co-religionists in our communities. But we have to go beyond the annual joint Thanksgiving Day services with church, synagogue, and mosque—as meaningful as these activities are. We need to learn about other faiths, particularly Islam, by experiencing the rituals of other traditions to cultivate an appreciation and an understanding that transcends mere tolerance. What does it mean—on a deep level—to be a Jew or a Muslim, a Hindu or a Buddhist? How can your congregation engage in sustained dialogue with other religious traditions to determine how we read sacred texts both similarly and differently? How does each tradition demonstrate love of the neighbor and hospitality to the stranger?

Such dialogue is not for the purpose of feeling good about the other or dispelling stereotypes, as important as these are, but making these connections, which will give you the partners you need to pursue justice and peace issues in your neighborhood and the world. Catholic theologian Paul Knitter reminds us that the suffering people in our world cry out for religious people to stop fighting and to join together to "feed the sheep." The goal, therefore, of multifaith dialogue is collaborative action.[5]

Ironically, the fourth and final strategy, becoming more rooted in your own tradition, flows from your own deeper appreciation for the religious other in your community. It may seem counterintuitive, but those involved in multifaith work commonly experience a deeper engagement in their own tradition. This is critical when you become a more visible public leader. When you find your place at the table and become one of those called upon to address a crisis or solve a problem, being able to draw wisdom and strength as well as insight from your own sacred texts and theological tradition is crucial.

Jewish theologian, scholar, and activist Abraham Joshua Heschel once described the spiritual discipline of being an activist in the civil rights movement with the image "We were praying with our feet." My hope for pastors and preachers everywhere is that we will claim and reclaim our roles as public leaders, as visible spokespersons for justice, as repairers of the breach, and as those who lead others with God's help in healing and repairing the world.

Notes

1. Elizabeth Lynn and Barbara G. Wheeler, *Missing Connections: Public Perceptions of Theological Education and Religious Leadership*, Auburn Studies 6 (New York: Auburn Theological Seminary, 1999).
2. Quoted in Katharine Rhodes Henderson, *God's Troublemakers: How Women of Faith Are Changing the World* (New York: Continuum, 2006), 53.
3. Quoted in ibid., 51.
4. Robert Wuthnow, "Responding to the New Religious Pluralism," *CrossCurrents* 58, no. 1 (Spring 2008).
5. Paul Knitter, *One Earth, Many Religions: Multifaith Dialogue and Global Responsibility* (Maryknoll, NY: Orbis Books, 1995).

12

Don't Take My Advice

JAMES C. HOWELL

In my wedding homilies, I frequently tell the worshipers (or perhaps they are merely "guests," hoping I will hurry so they can bolt for the party) something like this: "When you get to the reception, you will be tempted to whisper your pet advice on life and marriage to the bride or groom, but try to refrain from doing so, for each marriage is its own peculiar adventure."

I have been tempted by the editor of this volume to whisper advice on preaching or ministry, and I will refrain from doing so, since your vocation is unique, a novelty in time and space, challenging, fulfilling, and befuddling in ways you well understand. Any advice I'd hand you wouldn't fit, and might even be demoralizing. I have found ministry to be wonderful and terrible, and strangers I've read who dole out wise nuggets seem distant and unhelpful.

Besides, God wouldn't want you to be like me. I have fawned over a few great preachers, celebrities in the theological world, and have tried to mimic their moves and reproduce their achievements. Then one day I heard my daughter's voice from the back seat of the car, complaining in exasperation about her little brother: "He's copying me!" Yes, you grow by the imitation of others, but maturity perhaps is delayed until you learn to be who you are—until you become the one God made you to be.

Don't take too much advice from anybody. Be yourself. This is little understood, particularly in homiletics. I see clergy straining to be someone else, vaunting a preachy voice, dabbling in technique, only to realize that a filmy glass materializes between preacher and people, and the sermon becomes boring. The good news is that no preacher is stuck in the land of boredom. Every person I have ever met is interesting, intriguing, even downright strange, and you could spend a lifetime getting to know him or her. Be that person in the pulpit, not somebody else. Impersonators get stale fast.

So don't take my advice. Take your own advice. Talk to yourself. I do this in the car, in the shower, on the sidewalk, while biking. Garner the best conceivable advice by doing what I hope you did as a child: daydream. Once when I pressed my congregation for some semblance of Sabbath observance, one guy asked me, "So if Sunday is a day I don't do anything, then what will I do all day?" I laughed, and said, "Daydream." As a boy I climbed on top of a huge rock in the woods behind our house and whiled away afternoons daydreaming. It's good for children and good for clergy. Ideas float by; you get in touch with nature and yourself. You can simply *be*—something at which we clergy aren't very adept.

I would share something that strikes me as a bit curious. It may feel like advice, but it's more of a confession. We all need some foil for what we are about. We all are students of some tutor or another, even if in an accidental way. From whom have I picked up my cues for ministry and preaching? Not fellow preachers or even my elders and the most stellar exemplars of our craft. They haven't been half as helpful as those who aren't clergy at all. In fact, my imagination has been stretched and even blown away most often by advice from people who would say they have no advice at all about ministry and preaching; some would say they do not even believe in God.

My advice? My confession? Get outside the building, talk to people who aren't church insiders or experts, listen to those who think church is just so much tomfoolery, who are not agile spiritually, who don't quite get what you're up to. Of course, I could expostulate about this in some shrewd theological way: for instance, I could say Jesus connected with people in the world, not the religious insiders, and if we would be meaningfully evangelical or missional, we had better learn what outsiders are thinking.

But my thinking here isn't so hifalutin theologically. It's just the simple, embarrassing truth that clergy who talk about being clerical or preachers expounding upon homiletics bore me—and, unfortunately, I've been one of those boring others! It's just a fact that if I think about my work I find people in other professions doing the kind of thing I do better than I do; it's just a fact that if I think about preaching, I hear nonclergy talkers who do what I'm trying to do far better than I or other homileticians.

If you want to preach well, don't listen to sermons. Think about great speakers who aren't preachers. Winston Churchill mastered the spoken word, and he prepared diligently (frequently in the bathtub), writing not in paragraphs but in "psalm-form," which is the way people actually speak. Very deliberately he planned his fumbles, pauses, and scratches of the head, practicing endlessly in front of mirrors (frequently, as his butler and maid would attest, in the nude).

Turn on the television. Watch the lawyer make her closing summation to the jury. The facts are fuzzy, and so very much is at stake. How does she marshal what fragments are known, the potent emotion in the room, a raised eyebrow, the modulation of vocal volume and tone, to persuade a dozen people to acquit?

Watch a popular movie such as *Independence Day*. The president, played by Bill Pullman, grabs a microphone and rallies a bunch of ex-pilots to save the world with a rousing speech. Watch the memory of your own life: think back to the day that stranger you used to be took the hand of a young woman you were dating and declared, "I love you. Will you marry me?" Or maybe you were that woman chasing him until he finally caught you. Do that in the pulpit. Be the lover, the president, the lawyer, the suitor, and your preaching will soar.

If you want to manage your church effectively, absolutely do not listen to the church management gurus. Somebody in your congregation runs a family business, or manages a branch bank; somebody draws graphics for an advertising firm, or is the foreman for a team of brick masons. Explain to them the way we run our parishes, let them in on the structure our denomination mandates, and they will laugh out loud. Then they will tell you how to work a budget, how to connect with rude customers, how to corral and empower employees. Do whatever they tell you.

If you want to be a good theologian, read the theologians, of course. But find somebody who doesn't believe in God, somebody who thinks church is the crassest nonsense: the guy who got burned by the church and will never return, the woman who's into some spirituality you think is totally off the wall. Listen to these people, find out how they think; don't shut down their questions, but roll with them.

Abraham Lincoln was not much impressed by the clergy of his day, and he wasn't a diligent Bible reader. He had no training in theology, and yet his depth of understanding of God's heart and ways in the world are rarely matched by the trivialities we hear in most sermons. Whose side is God on in wars or politics or moral issues today? Lincoln stood between North and South and declared, "Both read the same Bible . . . but the Almighty has his own purposes."

We must read, of course. Stephen King gave this counsel to writers, which applies perfectly to preachers:

> It's hard for me to believe that people who read very little should presume to write and expect people to like what they have written. If you don't have time to read, you don't have time (or the tools) to write. I take a book with me everywhere I go, and find there are all sorts of opportunities to dip in. The trick is to teach yourself to read in small sips as well as in long swallows. Waiting rooms, theater lobbies, boring checkout lines, and everyone's favorite, the john. You can even read while you're driving, thanks to the audiobook revolution.[1]

Just think of the great work Luther managed on the john.

But beware the spewing of vapid books from our denominational publishing houses! How to preach snappy sermons? How to run a growing church? How to produce fantastic Christians? Read instead good theology, the kind that is hard to read and leaves you puzzled.

Then read just as much that is utterly nontheological. A New York restaurateur, Danny Meyer, wrote *Setting the Table*, in which he tells how the restaurant business isn't really about food, but about people, and how he motivates his staff to be hospitable, always listening, cajoling, making personal connections.[2] Pastors run something like a restaurant: we feature bread and wine, and it's all about people and hospitality.

Drawn to the title, I picked up Harry Frankfurt's brilliant little book whose title might make you blush: *On Bullshit*.[3] What should embarrass us isn't the profane word that appears so brazenly, but the phenomenon of BS and its hostile takeover of all talking and listening that goes on in our culture. The BSer, according to Frankfurt, isn't a liar; he doesn't care enough about truth to bother getting it wrong. The BSer simply will say anything to get you to do whatever he wants; the BSer is trying to talk you into something. The risk of BS in the pulpit is gargantuan, and people who listen have BS receptacles, if you will, ears cocked to hear precisely what they want to hear. My advice? Read Frankfurt, and then spend the rest of your life with your antennae raised, wary of BS coming out of your own mouth. Many in our congregations have good BS detectors and see right through us when we try to throw BS around.

Another lovely book bears the quirky title *Um . . . Slips, Stumbles, Verbal Blunders, and What They Mean*.[4] Michael Erard analyzes when and why people fumble, pause, misspeak, and drive compositional perfectionists to distraction. He outlines the virtues of stumbling and pausing, which demonstrate you are thinking, or maybe you're a bit unsure. Moreover, the listener has a little gap to pencil words in ahead of you, or to linger over the previous thought. I take considerable comfort in this as I get jammed up and ramble through incomplete sentences and jumbled thoughts while preaching.

Yet isn't this as it should be? If you took too much good advice, you could produce sentences of stellar quality, and your English teacher and a speech coach would give you an A+. But we're talking about God here. It's not advice, but I try to hold in my mind the single most wise thought I have ever heard about preaching: Karl Barth banished all BS when he said, "As ministers we ought to speak of God. We are human however, and so cannot speak of God. We ought therefore to recognize both our obligation and our inability and by that very recognition give God the glory."[5] We lap up advice thinking we can alleviate our inability. But this desire, however noble, is futile. And learning to accept this futility, to live with the obligation to fail, is the fulfillment of our vocation.

The failure of faith, I have come to believe, is little understood. People trash the church for being a silly shell of what it ought to be, but it is the flawedness of the church that leaves room for an incarnate Lord to meet silly shells of people who aren't who they ought to be. People feel a hollowness in their souls and wish the preacher could fill the tank with clever words, but the hollowness was placed there by a God who wants to be sought, not found. People are disillusioned with God and religion, and we celebrate, for disillusionment is nothing other than the shedding of illusions, the disposal of some BS we have harbored about God. For it is the true, living God—never cornered, forever mystifying, yet very real, tender, inescapable—that we serve, and we do so foolishly, as simpletons who could really use a lot of shrewd advice.

Notes

1. Stephen King, *On Writing: A Memoir of the Craft* (New York: Pocket Books, 2000), 142.
2. Danny Meyer, *Setting the Table: The Transforming Power of Hospitality in Business* (New York: HarperCollins, 2006).
3. Harry G. Frankfurt, *On Bullshit* (Princeton, NJ: Princeton University Press, 2005).
4. Michael Erard, *Um . . . Slips, Stumbles, Verbal Blunders, and What They Mean* (New York: Pantheon, 2007).
5. Karl Barth, *The Word of God and the Word of Man*, trans. Douglas Horton (New York: Harper & Row, 1956), 186.

13

You Don't Have All the Answers—
and That's Okay!

MARY LIN HUDSON

Don't be afraid of what you don't know. Instead, embrace "unknowing" as a gift for preaching. Staring at the blank page at the beginning of each sermon can become paralyzing at times. The thought of finding words time after time often leads the preacher into conversation with those haunting voices deep within: How can I preach when I'm out of words and I have nothing to say? How can I preach when I'm not even sure that the gospel is true? In a world of seemingly endless and empty words, is there anything left to say? The questions seem stifling at the beginning of the homiletical process. But what if these questions are really a gift to the preacher, rather than a curse? What if these questions are really a springboard to better preaching?

The privilege of preaching brings its moments of terror and doubt, especially in the face of difficult days and sometimes sleepless nights that are all too common for persons in ministry. In times like these the feelings of hesitancy, fatigue, and even anger that are present need to be acknowledged as reasonable responses to a world full of violence and suffering. If you aren't shaking your head in frustration or wiping tears from your eyes, perhaps you aren't paying attention to the death and confusion surrounding you. In moments like these, it seems that the most predictable posture of the preacher is to be sitting with head in hand or even fist in air, hoping for a word of God to break the silence. In moments like these, the preacher needs to hear a word from a source other than the conventional wisdom or clever rhetoric of the age. "Not knowing" is the first step to good listening.

Embracing the unknown frees the preacher to be human before God on behalf of the congregation. Moments of uncertainty in a preacher's life put her or him in touch with a place of vulnerability that makes the preacher unmistakably human. A friend who is both experienced and thoughtful in the pulpit was rehearsing her calendar engagements for the weeks just following Easter. "I'm speaking on Wednesday night, Thursday evening, and all day Saturday about the meaning of 'resurrection,'" she said. "The irony of it is that I'm not sure I even believe it anymore. I haven't seen God show up lately to defy the powers of death around me." At times like these, the preacher is stripped of superficial appeals to fairy-tale endings for the narrative of hope. The "alleluias" taste like cardboard on the tongue. Embracing doubt, the preacher has a chance to set aside the preformed apologetics of the traditional church and seek new language for a waiting humanity. Let honest doubt confront God and demand a response. Such confrontation takes God seriously and engages God honestly with expectation. It leaves us wrestling, like Jacob and the stranger, with the meaning and purpose of our lives.

The questioning preacher may name the human burden of faith in ways that people in the pews need to hear. Sermons that are reduced to sound bites are barely reassuring in a world out of control. Sermons that offer magical solutions to difficult problems can reduce God to a formula for happiness in a world that craves satisfaction. However, sermons that begin with the need for a candid answer and a new word from God may lead people to more honest engagement with the world and a more earnest desire to know God. Embracing the unknown is the first true step of faith. Embracing what you don't know frees the preacher to listen more carefully to the Scripture text. Scripture is a gift, not a tool. The biblical witness offers itself to the preacher as a lens through which she or he may view the landscape of the present world with eyes open to mystery and meaning. If a preacher assumes that he or she already knows what will be found there, the reading of the text becomes an exercise in analysis, rather than a journey toward discovery of a transforming word of liberation.

A few years ago, I had the rare privilege of spending my spring break on Eleuthera Island in the Bahamas. The breezes were warm, the sand was pink, and the weather was perfect. I was content to sit in my beach chair, reading novels and dozing hour after hour, soaking up the moments of bliss. I was content, that is, until I tried snorkeling. It took me a while to get comfortable in my gear—to learn how to breathe easily, keep my mask clear, and float without struggling. I fought the process for a long time, but then when I relaxed I entered a world that I had only read about in books. I swam along a coral reef, playing hide-and-seek with mysterious and amazing sea life that welcomed me into this new world. Such life had lain just beyond my toes for many hours, and I hadn't even recognized its presence. Now, through snorkeling, I had found a window into incredible wonder and complexity. It was only the sting of sunburn that reminded me of my own limitations and forced me to return to the shore. Today I love snorkeling, and I am open to any invitation to return to that amazing experience of beauty and peace.

Biblical exegesis should be as surprising and rewarding as snorkeling. Embracing the unknown allows the preacher to listen to the ancient witness with a naiveté that longs to hear what is being said. Knowledge leads to analysis, distancing us from any true encounter with the "other" that waits to be discovered. The suspension of knowledge can lead to a meeting with the other that changes us and our understanding of the world around us. Honest questions lead to more honest engagement of texts.

Embracing the unknown frees the preacher to concentrate on what is right in front of her or him, rather than reaching for an ideal that is too theoretical ever to imagine, much less live into. In a state of vulnerability, the preacher has little to prove and more to receive. As a result, the mundane, almost invisible world of daily life becomes more alive and revealing to the world of the sermon.

The ability to embrace one's own vulnerability allows us to lay down our swords and shields, to wade into the sea of common humanity and face the vulnerability of the other as a place of glory and grace. Instead of reaching for the rhetoric of the marketplace or the language of political discourse, the preacher is free to open herself or himself to the interpersonal expression that defies the dehumanizing language of dominance and submission. When the preacher has little to prove and more to receive, the smallest act takes on greater significance, and we discover that the God of distant galaxies has moved in "next door" to us.

For the past few years I've taught a course titled "Preaching on Contemporary Issues." In the course, participants are introduced to political, social, and economic issues that confront the church and the world. We look at current events and the rhetoric that shapes them in social consciousness. One of the primary challenges of the course, however, is learning how to move beyond the conventional reading of contemporary issues in order to recognize the presence and transforming power of God in the midst of them.

One way that participants try to engage in this contemporary approach to preaching is through an exercise of encounter with a human face that stands at the heart of an issue. Ideally, this encounter would be a face-to-face conversation in which the preacher is confronted by the different world of the other. Such an experience occurred one day when a class was on a field trip and happened to encounter a homeless man who asked for money. The interruption proved more productive than any lecture. In that encounter, all of the issues of economic privilege, socialization, theology, and vulnerability streamed together in honest confession and conversation. At first, an uneasy silence followed the face-to-face conversation. A few words were offered to break the silence, and then someone changed the subject. Later, however, the agenda of the class was set aside completely when the participants could not let go of their need to talk about the event. In a simple encounter, their conventional world of meaning was disrupted, and they needed to find words to reorder their understanding in light of that disruption. In the encounter with the human face on the street, a new word emerged.

Embracing the unknown may allow us to refocus our vision away from distant galaxies of meaning toward the stories, conversations, and foolish daily acts of earthly life today. Perhaps we will find God as close as a visit with our next-door neighbors.

Embracing the unknown may leave the preacher feeling pretty foolish and frustrated at times, but it opens up the pathway to new authenticity, vision, and vulnerability. These are gifts that free the preacher to experience and interpret the grace of God in a more profound way. Certainly, there are times when the preacher cannot grasp the meaning of the gospel and is called to speak beyond her or his own experience. In many ways, it would be so much easier for the preacher to settle weekly for a conventional word and simply mimic the language of Scripture and tradition. In many of those cases, a congregation might find comfort in the sound of those words. However, the comfort of the congregation should not set the standard for preaching. Instead, during those times when pressing questions of faith seem to wrestle down the answers, don't reach for somebody else's word for the gospel. Let the tears flow. Shake your fist at God. Go back to that glimpse of grace that you remember in your own life. Anchor yourself there, and then unpack your snorkeling gear. Preaching offers an opportunity to explore the vulnerability of this earthly existence, the surprising landscape of the world of the biblical text, and the disrupting presence of God in the next-door experiences of life. Don't be afraid of what you don't know. Instead, embrace it.

14

Imagination and the Exegetical Exercise

CLEOPHUS J. LARUE

An enduring criticism of American Protestant preaching, and especially the preaching in the mainline churches, is that on the whole it is too flat, too horizontal, too colorless—in a word, unimaginative.[1] It often lacks sparkle, intrigue, provocative thought, and mental images that help us to see and to say the Word in new ways. The preaching that so many of us are inclined to do is discursive, rationalistic, and given to simple outline form, as if that's all our people expect from us. Our creative energy goes into saying it quickly, quietly, and getting the gospel drudgery out of the way as soon as possible. More often than many of us would like to admit, we are, in a word, boring, speaking only because we *have to say something*, as opposed to speaking because we *have something to say*. Fred Craddock is right when he says, "It is unfortunate and unfair that imagination has been popularly allied primarily with fantasy and thus often spoken of pejoratively as 'just imagination' in the sense of the unreal and the untrue."[2]

Why is it the case that so much of our preaching is so lacking in imagination these days? Are we still reeling from the *Dragnet* effect of modernity—just "the facts ma'am, nothing but the facts"?[3] Or do we share John Calvin's fear of "pretty preaching" and therefore simply embark upon what many believe to be the unadorned, "plain style" preaching of the Puritan and Reformed tradition?[4] It may well be that the things that preclude us from imaginative and creative preaching are legion. Yet the question will not go away: How can we employ the imagination more effectively in service to the preached Word, to the God who came among us in the human flesh of a carpenter's son? What are we doing when we think imaginatively about the preached Word?

Imagination helps us see and say what often lies dormant within us. It is this seeing and saying that is so often lacking in biblical exegesis for sermon preparation. Frequently, the poet is silenced by the technician in an effort to get factual answers to those important exegetical questions. Unfortunately, however, somewhere in the exercise it dawns on the preacher that imagination has not been an active participant in the process. Only belatedly is the imagination invited in. Imagination is not simply a *step* in the exegetical process; neither is it an afterthought, an add-on, or a johnny-come-lately gloss on a point in need of further clarification. Imagination should permeate the entire exegetical exercise, because fertile creativity simply will not wait its turn to contribute to sequential, orderly exegesis. No wonder so many great ideas see the light of day on pieces of scrap paper, napkins, or the back of airline boarding passes. The imagination simply will not wait.

The only thing that should take precedence over openness to the imagination is our openness to the Spirit. And just as this openness to the movement of the Spirit cannot be assumed, but rather is eagerly sought and accepted on its own terms, so too is the imagination. The imagination will not be ordered around by any predetermined process. It is coauthor, not coeditor. It creates and calls forth. It does not merely review and rearrange. It is there throughout, impatiently insisting on a hearing. Imagination is at the crossroads of what Gardner Taylor calls that "mysterious romance between preparation and inspiration."[5] It involves a whimsical mixture of *seeing and saying*. Sometimes we can see it even when we can't say it. At other times vocalizing it helps us to see it better. Some experts on the inner workings of the brain maintain that humans use only about 10 percent of their brain power. No truer words have been spoken when one considers the untapped potential and limitless possibilities of our imagination. Before, during, and after formal preparation for preaching, the imagination is there pushing, cajoling, pressing its case, speaking into the preacher's ear and trying to gain a hearing if only the technical will occasionally yield to the poetic. The preparation process needs both. At their best, technician and poet are locked in a symbiotic relationship of creativity. During times of study, this interchange forces itself upon the preacher. The factual investigation is foremost only to defer and recede into the background as the poetic inference takes over.

It is clear from contemporary preaching manuals that an effective use of the imagination is not uppermost in the minds of many homileticians. Some homileticians don't even mention it, as if it has no place in the more technique-oriented exercise of sermon preparation. Others seem to suggest that it has a place, just not a very important one. Moreover, in all too many "how-to" preaching books, when the imaginative process is mentioned, what is meant to flow freely too often shows up as just another step in the exegetical exercise. Thinking imaginatively is not some slow, grinding process whereby you squeeze out some creative thought or idea after laborious exegesis. It takes work to craft the fruits of imagination into formal speech, but that comes when the sermon is written. The fresh burst of naked imagination that comes to us initially is different from the harvested fruits of imagination. Naked imagination at its best is a gift! It's like manna falling from heaven: you freely receive what is being given, knowing all the time that it is coming in such grand and gracious proportions that you simply do not have the wherewithal to receive it in full. No sermon is big enough or long enough to contain all that comes to us as imaginative gift in preparation for preaching. The gift of naked imagination is answered prayer: give us today what we need for today.

When the imagination is allowed to roam freely, our focus is not on trying to think up something new but on harvesting what has been given. Imagination at work looks more like a construction site rather than a ribbon-cutting ceremony: unused material is in abundance. In its spontaneity it is more akin to the brash child in the classroom who answers out of turn—though correctly—as opposed to the timid child waiting patiently with hand in the air. Imagination rushes past order. It is impatient with rules and regulations. Control freaks will always have difficulty with the quixotic emphasis inherent in imagination. Imagination roaming freely creates disorder and disarray. But out of that disorder springs forth ideas that would make the Athenians at the

Areopagus proud, for what comes forth is the hearing and telling of something new.

Trying to harness the imagination through theoretical definitions alone is the best way to hinder it. One of the worst things you can write is a boring book on the imagination. While there are many excellent writers who have thought through the theoretical implications of this process—Charles Rice, Thomas Troeger, and Paul Scott Wilson among them—theory alone will not unlock its treasures. Of course, one should read the theoretical books, but I also think it is important to begin the process of thinking imaginatively simply by accepting the process as a gift. Instead of focusing so much on how it comes, focus instead on the given that it will come. When it comes to receiving the imagination as gift, it's perfectly acceptable to be what the business world calls an "unconscious competent"—a person who knows how to do something but can't explain it to others. In the words of the apostle Paul, our task is to stir up the gift that is in us. The power to imagine is within you. The power to think through a text and use your imagination to create a sermon is within you. To know the source of the imagination is no guarantee that you will be the beneficiary of the end results of the imagination. Accept the gift and practice harnessing its creativity.

Three Ways to Harness the Imagination

How do you organize what is already within you? And how do you harness these free-flowing streams of continuous imaginative thoughts? There is no one set place, no particular "step," no fitting moment for the imagination in the exegetical process. However, imagination received as gift can and does revolve around three different poles: initial, informed, and enhanced.

Initial imaginative thoughts are probably the closest things to the first thoughts that come flowing from our innermost being. Sometimes these ideas flow from our lived experience before we even read a passage of Scripture. At such times it is experience in search of Scripture. At other times ideas flow when we reflect momentarily on a biblical passage as we remember it. Still at other times it a fresh reading of and/or a sustained focus on Scripture that stirs the imagination. Something in lived experience or in Scripture pricks the imagination, and the flow begins in earnest.

Initial imaginative thoughts may best be described as "unadulter-ated eisegesis." To engage in this reading into Scripture takes pluck. It takes resourceful courage and daring to think imaginatively, and to allow such thoughts to see the light of day. But the gains of such bold-ness could be worth well the risk. Even though initial imaginative thoughts grow out of our ignorance, sinfulness, sensuality, prejudices, and preferences, they still have a place in the process. They get us moving! They push us back from the jet bridge so we can taxi down the runway for our imaginative flight. This is true of Scripture and of life. Most exegetical exercises frown on eisegesis, since this reading into Scripture is thought to do a great disservice to what the text actu-ally means. Yet sometimes the most creative ideas happen just at this point of uninformed wonder. Because these initial, fleeting thoughts have a place in the homiletical process, I encourage preachers to entertain them and jot them down whenever and wherever they arise.

Informed imaginative thoughts are the reflections that grow out of thinking about what is actually in Scripture. This is the time in the exegetical exercise where you put yourself in conversation with the scholars and bring the formal tools of study to bear upon the process of discovering the meaning of the text. But here again, imagination should already be a part of the process. There is no need to invite it in. There are many good exegetical methods for helping preachers to gain a sense of the text and subsequently the claim of the text upon the hearers.[6] However, you don't put your imagination on hold when you are examining Scripture. I vehemently disagree with those who say informed reflection hinders the imaginative process. Informed reflec-tion unleashes your imaginative potential. It is when you really begin to understand what is going on in a text that the imagination places before you unlimited ideas and new ways of envisioning the text. Again, you move back and forth, if not on paper, most assuredly in your mind, between informed insight and imaginative possibilities. Even when one is searching through Bible dictionaries, monographs, and commentaries, the imagination is equally active in the search. Even if it's just an inkling of an insight, jot it down. Many of these fragmentary thoughts come to naught, while others find a place of prominence in the creation of the sermon. There are so many "aha" moments when the preacher is deeply involved in getting at the meaning of a text. One can almost hear the rush and feel the excitement of the imagination at work. Experienced preachers have the ability to separate the imaginative wheat from the chaff in their heads. However, in the early years of their preaching preparation, inexperienced preachers should simply write them down as they move through their investigatory process.

Enhanced imaginative thought. Imagination's work is never done, even when the sermon is as complete or as "pulpitworthy" as one has time to make it before the Sunday preaching hour. Let the imagination continue to work. Don't be afraid to add to your prepared manuscript. A written manuscript does not a sermon make. The manuscript is but an arrested performance that can only be brought to life through the living voice. Feel free to drop those pearls of great price as the imagination continues to produce even after you stand to preach, for even while you are preaching, the sermon is yet pregnant with imaginative possibilities. Temper it, of course, so that you don't go off on a tangent, but a sentence or two of insight that comes to you while preaching enhances the sermon and honors the imagination as it continues to work and place itself at the service of the preached Word. Even after the sermon has been preached and the imagination looks wistfully upon the sermon as past event, ideas continue to come. Jot them down on the manuscript. At some point you'll have an opportunity to preach that sermon or that passage of Scripture again.

Imagination is akin to the Spirit in that it blows where it will. It comes upon us as a sudden burst of illumination and powerful insight that defies being tamed or confined by the precision and accuracy of the written word. Imaginative bursts of insight are at once powerful and elusive, overbearing and fleeting. They come upon our mental horizon so forcefully that it is difficult at times to capture the faint glimmer of what just whisked past us. Some quickly vanish into our mental sea of reason and respectability, while others in their haste must be consigned to certain death. In such cases one can only hope that they will resurrect themselves on a slower day at a slower pace when we have once again opened ourselves to this great gift.

Notes

1. Gardner C. Taylor, *How Shall They Preach* (Elgin, IL: Progressive Baptist Publishing House, 1977), 60.
2. Fred B. Craddock, *As One without Authority* (Enid, OK: Phillips University Press, 1974), 77.

3. *Dragnet* was a television police show that aired in the 1960s and '70s. The lead character, Sgt. Joe Friday, played by Jack Webb, questioned his potential witnesses with this same admonition each week.

4. John H. Leith, *From Generation to Generation: The Renewal of the Church according to Its Own Theology and Practice* (Louisville, KY: Westminster John Knox Press, 1990), 89.

5. Taylor, *How Shall They Preach*, 58.

6. See Samuel D. Proctor, *The Certain Sound of the Trumpet: Crafting a Sermon of Authority* (Valley Forge, PA: Judson Press, 1994); Thomas G. Long, *The Witness of Preaching* (Louisville, KY: Westminster/John Knox Press, 1989), 60–77; Paul Scott Wilson, *The Four Pages of the Sermon* (Nashville: Abingdon Press, 1999); and Ronald J. Allen, *Interpreting the Gospel: An Introduction to Preaching* (St. Louis: Chalice Press, 1998), 119–50.

15

In Loco Pastoris

MICHAEL L. LINDVALL

L et me be clear, in fact blunt, about what the following
essay implies. It means that if you as a pastor cannot
come to love the congregation you serve, if you do not
love the culture and community in which that congregation is set, you
have to leave. And don't wait too long. Ministers cannot effectively
serve people whom they do not love. And if a pastor is ill at ease or at
odds with the culture of the larger community, the congregation will
soon come to recognize it and view their minister as the outsider that
he or she understands himself or herself to be.

I once attended a conference on the high plains of north central
Kansas. The landscape was stark and surreal: rolling prairie, waving
grasslands, and flint hills, but few trees—often no trees. I commented
on the strange loveliness of this to an older woman over coffee one
morning. She said, "Not everyone thinks it beautiful. I was on the pastor nominating committee for our church once. We had a candidate
we liked from New Jersey. I drove to the airport to pick him up. As we
headed west into the high plains and the trees got fewer and fewer and
the towns farther and farther apart, he began to get that 'deer in the
headlights' look in his eyes. He was talking less and less. Then we got
to the church for the interview and right in the middle of it, out of

nowhere, he just stood up and said, 'God would never call me to a place with so few trees. I want to go home now.'" Better now than later.

Conversely, when a congregation recognizes, as they invariably will, that their pastor loves them and loves their specific place in the world, his or her leadership, indeed authority, will almost always be eventually welcomed. I recall William Sloane Coffin Jr. making this point in a quip offered at a ministers' conference. He said that he had always been amazed at how much he could "get away with" (he meant politically controversial sermons and church programs) as long as his people knew he loved them and that he respected their opinions.

The legendary congressman from Massachusetts and speaker of the House, Thomas "Tip" O'Neill, famously opined that "all politics is local." Likewise, all ministry is local, even more so than politics. There is simply and obviously no such thing as "ministry in general"; it is always ministry in a *specific* geographical place, among *specific* people and in a *specific* culture. Every pastor is *in loco pastoris*.

Ministry and Incarnation

The specificity of ministry is precisely parallel to the scandalous specificity of the incarnation. The incarnation had to be, by definition, in a single individual person whose physical body was specifically short or tall, dark or fair, handsome or not. Likewise, incarnation was in Jesus *of Nazareth*, not Jesus *of everywhere*. Jesus was a Galilean Jew and not an Alexandrian Jew. He lived his incarnate life in one specific time and no other. All these particularities are just that—particular. We may like them; we may not like them. We may find them strange and disagreeable, or we may deem them intriguing and endearing. The point is that these are the particularities that God chose for the embodied revelation of Jesus Christ. Here's the sharp edge for this discussion: such divine choice of the particular implies God's great love for the very specificities that God has chosen to embody the divine. It does not mean that the specifics of Jesus' incarnation—his body, time, culture, geography—are more loved than other specifics, such as other human bodies, other periods of time, other cultures or landscapes. Rather, it means that all are greatly in and for their uniqueness.

Likewise, ministry is incarnationally specific. Ministry is rural, urban, or small town. Congregations are rich or poor, growing or shrinking, happy or dour. Buildings are lovely and leaky, too big or too small. Cultural contexts are sophisticated or homey, rural, small town, big city, Bach, or country and western. The incarnational point here is that each person, each congregation, each context is loved by God in and for its particular uniqueness. Likewise, a pastor is called to see his or her people with the same "lover's eye," to love them for what they are in and for their very peculiarities.

Pastor as Professional

There are two vocational metaphors used to speak of the relationship between pastor and congregation that can work to distance one from the other. Both images have some value, but they can become problematic. First, it is commonplace today to speak of pastors as "professionals." The word appropriately suggests education and specialization along the lines of a physician or an attorney. It may also imply something about social position—indeed, a measure of recognition for which many clergy in our post-Constantinian disestablishment long. To be a professional may also imply that you do your work well, in other words, "professionally."

These nuances might indeed be helpful ways to speak of pastoral ministry, but the term bears another implication. A "professional" is also a provider of services, and in providing such services, a professional is also called to keep what is often approvingly named "professional distance."

The implication is that a pastor as professional is a person educated to know things that others do not fully understand (say, biblical Greek or the mysteries of higher criticism), or trained in certain skills (say, pastoral counseling or group dynamics), which he or she then offers to the congregation, people who are less well educated theologically and untrained in the skills of "professional ministry." Understood this way, the image of pastor as professional can support a new and almost secular clericalism, a distinction and distance between "lay" and "clergy" that is not so much about how close you are to God as it is about how close you are to "knowing it all."

I have come to think that the term "professional" is best eschewed in speaking of pastoral ministry. Yes, it makes a fit point about education, but its implications about social status are mostly vain and self-aggrandizing, and the implication of special ministry skills and theological expertise does nothing so much as trivialize ministry into technique—a bag of tricks and arcane seminary gnosis. Such an understanding of pastor as professional can work to distance "pastoral service providers" from the congregations to which they proffer their sundry professional services.

Pastor as Prophet

A second metaphor popularly used to imagine pastoral ministry, which is sometimes appropriate but deeply problematic, is that of pastor as prophet. The church is clearly called to a prophetic role, but this role belongs essentially to the church as a whole—congregations, judicatories, as well as national and global ecclesiastical bodies. It refers to individual pastors insofar as they lead their congregations or denominations to find their common prophetic voice.

The prophetic metaphor for pastoral ministry becomes problematic when the most usual model of prophecy in the Old Testament, that of a prophet speaking for God to fallen Israel and calling the people back to covenant faithfulness, is recast in the church so that the pastor becomes the voice of God calling the fallen church back to faithfulness. The perils are obvious and potentially deadly to the relationship between pastor and congregation.

Rather than being called to a prophetic role against the congregation, pastors are called to a prophetic role *with* the congregation *against* injustice and unrighteousness—injustice and unrighteousness that are not simply "out there" in the world but in and among us, the people of God, the pastor most emphatically and clearly included.

In actual practice, this is a hard and fine line for pastors and preachers to walk. Using lots of first-person plural pronouns alone— "we" and "us"—in the sermon will not suffice. Pastors are called to candidly identify with the congregations they serve in both complicity and call. For instance, my hermeneutical mantra whenever a Sunday Gospel text offers up Pharisees and scribes is that in the sermon they have to be "us"—not "you, the congregation" but "me, the minister" as well. Pastors who have grown angry with the injustices and inequities of the world—angry with ministry, angry with their congregations, and angry with themselves—often scold their congregations, sometimes subtly, sometimes with aggressiveness clothed in clerical passivity. And when they do it, they typically justify it by donning the prophet's mantle, the wearing of which allows them to imagine that such behavior is not only acceptable but even courageous.

The prophetic call of the Christian faith is clear and at our core, but that call is not so much the pastor's call as it is the church's call. A congregation will not be led to answer it by any amount of badgering or scolding. If the members of a congregation have not answered a prophetic call God may have set before them, it will take a pastor time, love, and patience in order to grow with them, side-by-side, toward a shared and faithful answer.

Pastor as Lover

The metaphor of marriage has sometimes been used to speak of the relationship between pastor and congregation. It doesn't work very well. For instance, ministers seldom stay in one place forever, so when a pastor leaves, is it divorce? I am more drawn to the metaphor of lover and beloved, a younger cousin to the marriage metaphor, and one that is not without its own shortcomings. But there is one edge to the lover and beloved image that draws me to it. In my experience, people in love always seem to see the one they love in a way I can only call "hopefully." This is what I mean: lovers are not so much blind as they are somehow empowered by love to see their beloved with hope. Time and again in my experience, lovers clearly see the flaws and weaknesses of their beloved, but they somehow see those very imperfections as winsome, endearing, and full of promise. This, of course, is precisely the way God sees you and me, *simul justus et pecator,* "saint and sinner at the same time." And this is, I have come to believe, precisely how a pastor ought to love his or her congregation. You see all their flaws and weaknesses, but even those imperfections are somehow at the same time attractive, endearing, and full of promise.

When I accepted my first call as a pastor, my wife and I left our native Midwest for the decidedly foreign shores of Long Island. Everyone I talked to cautioned me about Long Island—the traffic, the rudeness, the accent, the price of housing. Long Islanders, I soon learned, picture the country as consisting of three islands—Long Island, Manhattan, and the large island to the west. When we arrived, we felt as though we had landed on the far side of the moon. The major social event of the year was the church clambake. I have a shellfish allergy, but I learned to love clambakes anyway. I discovered that the institution in town that commanded the strongest loyalties was the volunteer fire department. I became the fire department chaplain. It took a few years, but I even came to love the accent. Leaving was agony.

More recently we moved to Manhattan—I a native of the Upper Peninsula of Michigan, a "Yooper," and my wife an Indiana Hoosier. We found ourselves jolted again: Upper East Side money and East Harlem poverty side by side, the private schools, the men's and women's clubs, dinner parties where "informal" means coat and tie instead of a tux, an assumption of entitlement among some. It's a strange world to us and in so many ways a place with unique flaws and imperfections. But again, I can only see them through a lens of hope and love, even somehow winsome and appealing, and very full of promise. Already I find myself making it my place. I went out and bought a tux on sale at Macy's. I love New York. There is no other choice.

Love and Will

In premarital counseling sessions and wedding meditations, I tirelessly remind brides and grooms that love is a two-sided coin. On one side of the coin, I tell them, is how you feel—your passion for each other, that visceral and uncontrollable set of emotions that draw you to one another. But on the other side of the coin is what you choose—the choice you make to love. This is an act of will, commitment, and covenant. Feelings have sunny days and overcast days. The commitment you promise this day will pull you through the cloudy ones. Jesus commands just this kind of chosen love. Feelings can hardly be ordered up, but choices can indeed be commanded. So a pastor can and must choose to love his or her congregation. A pastor can and must choose to love the place in which he or she has been called to serve.

When we moved to New York City and I was finding my way into an unfamiliar congregation and very strange culture, I asked a long-term and successful former associate pastor of the congregation for advice. She offered me strange counsel, which I turned over and over in my mind and finally concluded was downright sage. "Have fun with it," she said. Take delight in it for what it is. Don't let it swallow your soul, but take pleasure and joy in it. Love the place, love the church, love the people, *simul justus et pecator.* You have no other choice, of course.

16

Keeping Your Eye on the Ball

Wisdom for Preachers from
the Splendid Splinter

THOMAS G. LONG

> God gets you to the plate, but once you're there, you're on
> your own.
>
> —Ted Williams

Most teenagers probably dream of becoming rock stars, video game designers, or the CEO of Google. Not Ted Williams, who from the time he was in high school yearned to be known as the greatest baseball hitter of all time. Not the greatest baseball *player*, mind you, but the greatest *hitter*, an obsession made all the more grand by the heat of its intense focus. "All I want out of life," he once said, "is that when I walk down the street folks will say, 'There goes the greatest hitter who ever lived.'"[1]

Whether he was or wasn't is a matter of debate, as it is with almost everything else in baseball. Some would say the irascible Ty Cobb was baseball's greatest pure hitter, others the irrepressible Babe Ruth, and still others the stained but nevertheless overpowering Barry Bonds, but a good case can be made that the "Splendid Splinter," as Williams was often called, achieved his dream. He hit for high average (.344 lifetime average), he hit for power (521 home runs in a career twice interrupted by military service), and, most impressively, he is the last man in the major leagues to hit over .400 in a season (.406 in 1941).

For nearly seven decades, no one, not even any of the bionic products of the Nautilus-trained, steroid-enhanced generation that followed Williams has toppled that record.

One thing is certain, though. Whether or not Ted Williams was baseball's greatest hitter, he was surely the game's greatest student of hitting. He literally wrote the book on hitting a baseball.[2] He ceaselessly analyzed grips and stances, fretted constantly about pitchers and their "stuff," and replayed endless loops in his mind of every at bat, especially his failures. It is here that Ted Williams, odd as it may seem, has much wisdom to offer preachers. Like hitting a baseball, preaching is often described as an "art." It is a nearly mystical and somewhat athletic performance that turns ordinary language and gesture into inspired and embodied sacred speech, an alchemy accomplished only by the truly "gifted" and the "anointed." Yes, there is art and mystery and anointing in preaching, but Williams would remind us that preaching, like hitting, is also a *craft*. There are techniques to learn, skills to be mastered, approaches to be studied, paths of excellence to be discovered and followed. Preachers are, of course, empty vessels, dependent upon the mercy of God, unable to preach the gospel unless the Spirit fills them up with the Word. But the Word always becomes flesh, always takes on a form that can be apprehended and comprehended.

When athletes are interviewed after a remarkable game or match, they will often say something opaque and cliché-ridden like, "I guess I was just in the zone today," or even more impenetrably, "During the whole game I was able to stay within myself." Nonsense, Williams would say. It is quite remarkable how little Williams, as a hitter, stayed "within himself." Good hitting, he knew, was a complex algorithm of concrete knowledge and specific skills. It was "out there" and available to be studied, learned, and mastered. "If there is such a thing as a science in sport," he said, "hitting a baseball is it."[3]

Preaching is not a "science," of course, and almost every experienced preacher can report occasions when she or he was "in the zone," when the preacher rode the crest of the Spirit's wave and proclaimed a Word well beyond that which could be accounted for by wit and skill. The temptation inherent in such experiences, though, is to make them definitive of practice, to allow them to encourage haphazard preparation and inattention to the fine details of excellence in the pulpit. It is one thing for preachers who have rigorously studied biblical texts, carefully honed the words and shapes of their sermons, and given thoughtful attention to body and gesture to find themselves exhilarated and humbled by becoming vessels of a Word beyond their mere human capacities. It is quite another for them to wander around the chancel with a wireless mike, a cheerful personality, and a thimble full of advance thought, holding their finger in the air and praying for lightning to strike.

In a mood somewhat playful but quite serious at the same time, let us look at some of the wisdom Ted Williams had about his own complex craft of hitting a baseball, to see if there are cognate insights about our craft of preaching.

"Much of your preparation is a matter of being observant, of picking up things. . . . What you're doing is building a frame of reference to work from."[4] Ted Williams observed everything. If a pitcher drew a bigger breath before letting loose a fastball instead of a changeup, or if the shortstop had a tendency to step forward when the catcher signaled for a curve, Williams saw it and filed it away. Hitting, he knew, is not simply a matter of putting the bat on the ball. The inevitable trajectory of the ball and the necessary arc of the bat are products of a complex interactive environment, and good hitters notice it all, from the stance of the center fielder to the direction of the breeze.

So it is with preaching. Good preachers keep their eyes open. The hungers, anxieties, and needs of the congregation and the culture are on full display to the watchful eye. "My parish!" exclaims the priest in Georges Bernanos's *The Diary of a Country Priest.* "The words cannot even be spoken without a kind of soaring love. . . . I know that my parish is a reality, that we belong to each other for all eternity; it is not a mere administrative fiction, but a living cell of the everlasting Church. But if only the good God would open my eyes and unseal my ears, so that I might behold the face of my parish and hear its voice."[5]

Notice, in this portion of Heidi Neumark's sermonlike *Breathing Space*—a memoir in which she describes her ministry in a tiny Lutheran congregation in the poverty-soaked South Bronx—how she *sees* things and uses what she sees to evoke the reality of her parishioners' life:

> Urban planning for the South Bronx began to cause the shrinkage of breathing space. . . . When you live in this community,

breathing space is not a figurative expression referring to longed-for leisure amid a hectic lifestyle. Breathing space is a matter of life and death. In the South Bronx more children die of asthma than almost anywhere else in the nation. Children pack asthma pumps in their pockets the way other kids pack action figures.

. . . As I got ready to lead worship for the first time, I noted that under the altar, a box of rat poison was set alongside a box of Communion wafers. The baptismal font was pushed back into a back corner and kept covered. I lifted the lid to discover a film of dust and the remains of a few dead cockroaches. Paradise had become a desert, and I felt like I had stepped inside of Sarah's womb.[6]

Asthma pumps in children's pockets, a box of rat poison next to the Communion wafers, a film of dust and dead cockroaches in the baptismal font—these images evoke a mood, an ethos, a place, a condition. Heidi Neumark is paying attention and, as Ted Williams advised, "building a frame of reference" that gives her writing (and her preaching) traction.

"Don't be distracted by the pitcher's moves, even if he's unorthodox. Focus on that area where his pitches usually come from."[7] Williams knew that pitchers could often make hitters look foolish by appearing to do one thing when actually doing another. Lefty Randy Johnson, for example, at 6 feet 10 inches tall, is all arms, legs, and whirligigs, and he is effective as a pitcher because his sidearm windmill delivery frequently fools batters, making it appear as if the ball is coming at them from first base instead of the mound.

Congregations can often fool preachers as well. Take a poll, and many congregants would say they want sermons on good parenting, keeping life balanced, and finding satisfaction and happiness in relationships. Important as these topics may be, we should not "be distracted by the pitcher's moves" but should pay attention to what truly matters, to the place where the "pitches usually come from." A desire to lure the preacher toward dispensing helps and hints for successful living often masks a desire for the holy vocation people hunger for and tremble before but dare not name: the call to be a disciple, the whitewater adventure of serving God by following Christ. Karl Barth warned preachers of his own generation not to be distracted. The preacher may think that the people in the congregation come wanting to know about symphonies and cherry trees, but, consciously or unconsciously, they actually leave behind all mundane concerns in favor of the one question that bursts forth like a flame: "Is it true? Is it true?" Is the claim that we stand in the presence of the living God to be believed, trusted, and lived?[8] Good preaching keeps its eye on the ball and, regardless of the particular subject of a given sermon, never loses sight of the fact that how people stand in the presence of the God of Jesus Christ is the one true theme of all Christian preaching.

"To me, the ideal swing has always been one that is slightly up."[9] This piece of hitter's advice from Williams is both unconventional and controversial. The accepted wisdom about hitting is that batters should strive to have a *level* swing. "I used to believe it, and I used to say the same thing," confessed Williams, but the notion that level swings were best was one of "a collection of mistaken ideas that batters parrot around."[10]

When it comes to preaching, the conventional wisdom among many preachers is that sermons should be up . . . way up. Since at least the time of Emerson and Beecher, American Christianity has been consumed with the desire to be overwhelmingly positive. "The power of positive thinking," "the possibility gospel," "your best life now!" and "the prosperity gospel" are but different incarnations of the same upbeat, God-wants-you-to-soar message, and as such constitute homiletical uppercuts.

Sometimes more thoughtful preachers have overreacted to the chipper enthusiasm of popular preachers by generating sermons that were, in effect, downswings. A desire to produce prophetic, counter-cultural preaching sometimes led preachers to assume a sober, doleful, heavy voice of grim responsibility. Williams's wisdom is sound for preaching too: the ideal sermon is one that is slightly up, one that recognizes that the gospel is, after all, the *good* news of God's redemption, but one that does not shy away from the shadow side of life and the hard realities of living the faith. "Is it all right to have a praise band in worship?" a seminary student asked his worship professor. "Yes," replied the professor, "but only if you also have a lament band."

"They talked for years about the ball being dead. The ball isn't dead, the hitters are."[11] Recently I wrote a short piece for the

Christian Century on pulpit plagiarism, focusing particularly on the regrettable practice of many clergy in "borrowing" sermons off of the Internet instead of crafting fresh ones for their specific congregations.[12] The article generated a fair number of letters to the editor, many with good responses and helpful critiques of what I had said. Several of the letters, however, expressed a troubling attitude on the part of the clergy who penned them—namely, that preaching was somehow passé and that anything that could make more efficient work of the chore of sermon preparation, including ripping off material from others, would save time for more important aspects of ministry.

There is nothing new about such thoughts. Periodically, clergy lose faith in preaching and begin to wonder if they could waste their time any more effectively than in preparing and preaching sermons. A severe depression in preaching stock occurred, for example, in the early 1970s, with the result that many seminaries reduced or even dropped their required courses in preaching.

Significantly, the recurrent pessimism about preaching is almost always a function of the clergy, not the laity. Even when they have been numbed into submission by years of boring, irrelevant, and incompetent preaching, lay folk seem able to hang on to the hope that the next preacher, or perhaps even the next sermon, will breathe of passion and life.

"The ball isn't dead," said Williams, "the hitters are." In his marvelous book *Confessing Jesus Christ*, homiletician David J. Lose surveyed the troubled landscape of Christianity in the postmodern American context, recording many dire assessments and dreary predictions of the demise of the church and the pulpit along with it. Taking full stock of this malaise, Lose nonetheless states:

> While I agree that the situation is clearly urgent, I am less sure that it is either dire or novel. In fact I am increasingly convinced that within the postmodern whirlwind there lies, waiting to be reaped, an unprecedented opportunity to clarify the nature and import of our theology and preaching.
>
> . . . *I propose that preaching that seeks to be faithful to the Christian tradition and responsive to our pluralistic, post-*

modern context is best understood as the public practice of confessing faith in Jesus Christ.[13]

In order to engage in the "public practice of confessing faith in Jesus Christ," however, preachers will need to have such faith and the courage to express it boldly and publicly. The hitter has to "stay alive" at the plate.

Ted Williams, the master of his craft, has a wealth of wisdom for preachers. It is a comfort, though, to hear the man who once batted over .400 reassure us that "baseball is the only field of endeavor where a man can succeed three times out of ten and be considered a good performer." I am not sure what constitutes a "good average" in the pulpit, but I do know that the sermons of even the most accomplished preachers are up and down, and that this rhythm of preaching is itself a witness to the contours of the Christian life. The journey of discipleship is a pilgrimage, not a ceremonial victory lap, and faithful preaching itself takes the long, steady pilgrim path of valleys and peaks. The goal is not to become a pulpit "star," a hideous concept on the face of it. The goal, rather, is not to lose faith in the God who summons us to this place, and once we are there, to employ all that we have been given in the practice of our craft. As John Updike said of Ted Williams, "For me, Williams is the classic ballplayer of the game on a hot August weekday, before a small crowd, when the only thing at stake is the tissue-thin difference between a thing done well and a thing done ill."[14]

Notes

1. Quoted in John Updike, "Hub Fans Bid Kid Adieu," *Baseball Almanac* online edition, http://www.baseball-almanac.com/articles/hub_fans_bid_kid_adieu_article.shtml. This essay first appeared in the *New Yorker*, October 22, 1960.
2. Ted Williams and John Underwood, *The Science of Hitting* (New York: Simon & Schuster, 1986).
3. Ibid., 12.
4. Ibid., 23.
5. Georges Bernanos, *The Diary of a Country Priest* (New York: Carroll & Graf, 1983), 28.
6. Heidi Neumark, *Breathing Space: A Spiritual Journey in the South Bronx* (Boston: Beacon Press, 2003), 7, 9–10.

7. Williams and Underwood, *Science of Hitting*, 14.
8. Karl Barth, "The Need and Promise of Christian Preaching," in *The Word of God and the Word of Man* (Boston and Chicago: Pilgrim Press, 1928), 108.
9. Williams and Underwood, *Science of Hitting*, 63.
10. Ibid., 13.
11. "Ted Williams on Hitting," unpublished sound recording.
12. Thomas G. Long. "Stolen Goods: Tempted to Plagiarize," *Christian Century* 124, no. 8 (April 17, 2007).
13. David J. Lose, *Confessing Jesus Christ: Preaching in a Postmodern World* (Grand Rapids: Eerdmans, 2003), 3; emphasis in the original.
14. Updike, "Hub Fans Bid Kid Adieu."

17

Preaching

Some Affirmations and Admonitions

JENNIFER LORD

I t is sabbatical time. I have had a few months away from the normal patterns of daily work and have been living in a different place with alternative ways of marking the days. In addition, I have inserted myself into a particular worshiping assembly as a visitor. It is a rich time with the community; I notice similarities to and differences from those patterns of worship familiar to me. Over these months I have come to count on one particular and unfamiliar action to bring me to attentive stillness. At this Orthodox Sunday liturgy (the Divine Liturgy), at the time of the reading of the Gospel, the small, eminently movable reading-preaching desk (*ambo* or *analoy*) is placed so that the deacon stands in the midst of the assembly, facing the iconostasis and the priest.[1] At this place the little building is octagonal and the deacon truly stands near the center.

There has been preparation for this moment—the little entrance that is a procession of the Gospel book by the priest, deacon, and servers through the congregation; the singing of the Trisagion;[2] the Peace at the end of the Trisagion; the reading of the Epistle with all the prayers and responses around the reading. These actions call the assembly to attend now to this moment when the Gospel is read, indeed proclaimed. The analoy is placed, the deacon moves to stand at the analoy, and the altar servers carry the candle and processional fans to surround the event of reading. The liturgy proceeds with these words, some spoken, some sung:

Priest: *In your love for mankind, Master, flood our hearts with the spotless light of your divine wisdom and open the eyes of our mind that we may grasp the message of your good news. Instill within us an awe for your blessed commandments, so that, overcoming all the cravings of our flesh, we may enter into a spiritual way of life, pleasing you in all our thoughts and actions. For you are the enlightenment of our souls and bodies, Christ, our God, and we give glory to you, your eternal Father, and your all-holy, good, and life-giving Spirit: now and forever, and unto ages of ages.* (spoken)

Choir: Amen.

Deacon: Bless, Master, him who proclaims the good tidings of the holy Apostle and Evangelist (Matthew, Mark, Luke or John the Theologian).

Priest: May God, through the prayers of the holy, glorious, and all-laudable Apostle and Evangelist _____, enable you to proclaim the good tidings with great power, to the fulfillment of the gospel of His beloved Son, our Lord Jesus Christ.

Deacon: Amen. Wisdom! Let us attend. Let us listen to the Holy Gospel.

Priest: Peace be unto all.

Choir: And to your spirit.

Deacon: The reading from the Holy Gospel according to Saint _____.

Choir: Glory to Thee, O Lord, glory to Thee.

Priest: Let us attend!

(The appointed Gospel lesson is chanted by the
deacon. Upon its completion the priest blesses
the deacon.)

Priest: *Peace be unto you who have proclaimed the
Gospel.* (spoken)

Choir: Glory to Thee, O Lord, glory to Thee.[3]

The assembly joins in the choir responses and sings those words
familiar in variation to many Western Christians: "Glory to Thee, O
Lord, glory to Thee." This little temple, octagonal shaped and without seating, houses a bit more chaos than my familiar basilica-style
building with pew rows fixing us into our places.

In the midst of the placement of the analoy, people moving to face
the gospeler, and the antiphonal responses, the deacon assumes a posture. He stands at the small desk in our midst, holds the Gospel book
in both hands with its bottom edge resting on the upper edge of the
desk, and then he bends his neck and rests his forehead on the top
edge of the Gospel book.

His neck is bared.

What can this mean? Our liturgical postures and gestures carry and
make meaning, whether or not the intention is there on our part.
Here is an intentional action. It is a carefully repeated action, always
at the same time during the Divine Liturgy, beginning at the moment
of the deacon's petition for the priest's blessing upon him.[4] The deacon moves out of this posture at the completion of that blessing.

It is a posture of submission by the deacon to something greater
than himself. Yes, he is the one who will chant the Gospel; it is his
voice that will physically make the Gospel reading audible that day in
the assembly's midst. The power of proclamation is his but not his,
and he bows his head and bares his neck to God, who enables his
proclamation. This makes sense. Though not a prayer addressed
directly to the Holy Spirit (and, in Orthodox tradition, a prayer that
concludes by calling upon the Gospel writer as a saint to intercede),
it is still a prayer calling upon the power of God to make this reading
the proclamation of the glad tidings of Jesus Christ. Here is something recognizable for Western Christians: just as we bow our heads

in prayer (at blessing), so the deacon's head is bowed in prayer because he is receiving a blessing.

This bowed head, neck-bared pose represents the posture of vulnerability. We know that some persons of lower class status bow their heads before kings and superiors. And this—if your superior is not pleased with you, your head may be cut off. This bared-neck position is the posture of a person, head down, at the sword. It is not a position of strength or control.

After the reading, the priest blesses the deacon saying, "Peace be unto you who have proclaimed the gospel." Peace is a welcome blessing after being in a dangerous posture. Then the priest (sometimes the deacon) preaches the sermon.

What is a Presbyterian to make of the posture in this Orthodox Divine Liturgy, and what difference does it make? My answer—affirmation and admonition—comes from another ecumenical relationship.[5] It's a principle used by some Christians to study each other's actions and doctrines, and to engage in learning and in the upbuilding of the body of Christ.[6] For this essay, here is my question: What does this liturgical posture of bowed head and bared neck affirm and admonish about preaching?[7]

Affirmation: We know this bow of blessing and vulnerability, for it is akin to the Protestant Reformed tradition's insistence on a prayer of epiclesis before the reading of Scripture and the preaching of the gospel. We do not move immediately from the gathering rite (call to worship or opening sentences, prayer of the day, hymn, confession and pardon) to the reading of the Old Testament or the Epistle or the Gospel. We first pray a specific type of prayer. It is not a prayer of thanksgiving or intercession but a prayer calling on the power of the Holy Spirit to enliven our reading and preaching (and hearing and living). This particular prayer announces our reliance on the reality of divine agency, on the triune One who is other than us and at the same time at work through our efforts.

Affirmation: We know about gathering around the word in our midst. We too turn our attention to the reading and proclamation of the Word of God. Even in Western Protestant contexts, secondary actions take place around the reading and proclamation of the Word. Some of our churches retain similar antiphonal sentences between reader and choir or assembly. More often the choir sings an anthem at this juncture. Sometimes the children come forward for a children's message. These actions around the word serve to demarcate that part of the service. They are actions that help say, "Now is the time to be gathered into the Scriptures!"

Affirmation: We know this posture of vulnerability before the Holy One. We believe that God chooses to give away life through the very stuff of study, preaching, and hearing. We rely upon God to make this happen. But we are responsible too. We make good use of creaturely gifts of study, knowledge, and diligence. We make good use of interpretation in community. Yet sometimes preachers fall short and do not preach the present grace of God. And some communities do not rightly divide the word of truth. Even in our responsibility we are vulnerable. We recognize a bow before God and one another.

Affirmations bring admonitions, because by affirming a deep truth, we also reveal an attentiveness that is needed. Pay attention to the image of this posture: I believe it brings fresh clarity and warnings. This posture at the Gospel reading informs our preaching.

Admonition: Do not hide true words. We all have them. But we end up speaking so many less-than-true words. Because of our nervousness, or our hubris, or our inattention, we don't always get to the important words. Instead we use self-deprecating remarks (which point to the preacher); we use sardonic humor (that says we are smarter than the listeners); we tell jokes (which point again to the preacher and are different from showing inherent humor in the texts); we use filler (instead of honing our words); we keep company with clichés and analogies that aren't weighty enough for pulpit speech (to speak of the death and resurrection of Jesus Christ for the life of the world). Even our self-disclosure can get in the way because it is another way to focus on the preacher's self. Look at those sentences of the Liturgy again: the petitions, blessings, and responses are words with weight. Get to the true words—say those things that will really matter for our faith, for our lives.

Admonition: Bring us word-of-life preaching, not a to-do list. Do not let your words only say what we should/ought/must do. Feed us with words of life. We yearn to come again to faith, a faith that stands honestly alongside the world's goodness and dis-grace. We all need to be converted even more deeply. We need new life every day. A prescriptive list does not do this. In the deacon's sung proclamation there is an assuredness that God is active and present. Let your words be a verbal icon, too, speaking Christ present in our midst and present to all the needs of the world.

Admonition: The preaching is both not you and you. The deacon asks for the blessing and bows his head during the blessing. He too prays that he will be enabled by the power of God to make right proclamation of the gospel. The "not him" is emphasized as the priest, the choir, and the whole assembly (including all the saints) invoke God's activity in the moment. At the same time the "him" is prominent. Someone must bring the gospel to hearing; we need a person to speak (chant) the word and sing and pray that he will do so. This deacon has prepared for this moment.[8] Then he proclaims it. The deacon in that moment stands in a tensive space, between humility and subjectivity, and authorized responsibility. We preachers don't always live well in that space: we too often exchange humility and subjectivity for self-doubt and fear, and exchange authorized responsibility for bravado and ego preening. But here, this deacon-priest-choir-assembly dialogue can be a cautionary moment: it is always both not about us and about us. In the midst of the assembly we seek the balance to live well in that space.

Admonition: To the weary preachers: listen to the whole assembly, seen and unseen, praying for you. We surround you. We join voices to call strength and ability upon you. We are admonished to pray for you. To the worn-out ones: the deacon's forehead rests on the Gospel book. God sustains in the midst of the community.

And here is one more admonition, but it is one that reaches beyond the preaching moment. It is an admonition that we look again at our worshiping order. How do our rituals of reading relate to the preaching event? The small things become big: well-trained readers who are clear, audible, assured; prayers that are about more than the preacher's nerves; a recovery of antiphonal sentences around the readings that serve to emphasize the involvement of the hearers; choices of music that ready us for the readings. In this time in our services, in setting out verbal icons, help us to be attentive.

Preaching work is "outstretched neck" work. It is right to be aware of great vulnerability. Here is an image of one posture borrowed from these Orthodox sisters and brothers in Christ. It is a moment of the assembly's attention and waiting, the singing, the blessing, the supplication, all toward the right sense of expectation that there will be a word of life for us this day.

Notes

1. The iconostasis is the stand or screen of icons and is not a barrier (though it demarcates altar from nave) but is an invitation to communion with the church triumphant. This congregation is Byzantine rite, part of the Orthodox Church in America. The priest stands behind the iconostasis just to the right of the "High Place" or "Teaching Place," the center being reserved for the bishop.
2. "Holy God! Holy Mighty! Holy Immortal! Have mercy on us" (sung three times).
3. *The Divine Liturgy according to St. John Chrysostom*, 1967, 2nd ed. (South Canaan, PA: St. Tikhon's Seminary Press, 1977), 41–43.
4. This posture is prescribed in the Russian Orthodox Church.
5. *A Formula of Agreement*, adopted in 1997, declares full communion between the Evangelical Lutheran Church in America, the Presbyterian Church (U.S.A.), the Reformed Church in America, and the United Church of Christ. The theological conversations that led to entrance into/affirmation of full communion made use of this working principle ("mutual affirmation and mutual admonition"), allowing for edification and correction of each other toward doctrinal consensus. See http://www.elca.org/ecumencial/fullcommunion/formula/official_text.html.
6. In this brief essay I am not a partner in dialogue as suggested by the principle, but I make use of it in a heuristic manner. I will not affirm or admonish the Orthodox practice (though note here obvious gender-leadership and language differences); this work may begin a conversation that serves longer discussion in another venue. This beginning of a ritual reading is my own. I am thankful to the most gracious and learned Very Reverend Stephan Meholick, Rector of St. Nicholas, San Anselmo, California, and the Reverend Deacon George Golitzen for conversation about these observations.
7. I ask this of preaching as I have experienced it in recent years in Presbyterian contexts but also in other Protestant, nondenominational, and postdenominational bodies.
8. This deacon studies the text in Greek, Latin, and Church Slavonic before reading it in the Divine Liturgy.

18

Preaching *From, With,* and *For*

JOHN S. MCCLURE

We are surrounded today by many voices promoting homiletical programs and ministerial agendas. Publishers and conference managers know what sells, and we want to keep up with the newest techniques. Our mailboxes fill daily with invitations to preaching conferences, book catalogs, DVD advertisements, and subscription offers. We feel pressured to join a particular movement, preach like certain well-known preachers, or subscribe to success-oriented approaches to ministry. In today's context, for instance, we worry that we are not countercultural, purpose-driven, emergent, or missional enough. Although many of the new "outside the box" programs do have good things to offer, we may wake up one day and discover that by "following the leader" we have lost much of our ability to be faithful and prophetic leaders in our own particular place and time.

The advice I offer below is meant to help you begin to live into your role as preacher in your own particular context. I want to encourage you to embed your preaching in the work that God is already doing where you are, so that you might lead and preach *from* that place. My goal is that you develop better ways to preach *from, with,* and *for* your actual congregation and community.

See your congregation and community as partners in proclamation. My first advice is that you begin to change how you see the people who participate in your sermons with you: your listeners. Instead of viewing them through any of the usual lenses as people in need of a new program or vision, resistant learners, lives waiting to be rescripted, or a collection of needy individuals in search of hints and helps for daily life, I encourage you to see them as co-journeyers, trustworthy *partners* in proclamation, and co-agents of the preaching task before you. Treat them as trainees, like you, in the school of prophetic proclamation, people who have a baptismal vocation and responsibility to give testimony and speak about the God who has saved them and is at work in their lives.

Preach collaboratively. How can we empower laity as proclaimers of the Word? One tried-and-true method is one that I call "collaborative or roundtable preaching." Here's how it works. Invite a small group to help you with your sermon brainstorming. This is not a clergy group of trained exegetes, as helpful as that might be. This is a weekly gathering of laypeople from within and beyond the church who discuss with you the biblical text for the upcoming Sunday sermon as it relates to their daily lives and the world in which they find themselves. Keep the group very small, three to four at a time at most. Change the group regularly, every couple of months, so that it doesn't become an in-group promoting its own agenda in the pulpit. Look on it as an expanding roundtable that grows and changes organically. One great way to keep the group expanding is to use a "tag team" method, in which each person rotates off the group after a specific length of time and must "tag" someone else, either within or beyond the church, as a replacement for the next two months. Challenge those who are leaving the group to find people who will bring something different to the group, something that was not represented during their tenure. This could be a difference in age, race, class, status in the congregation, or even someone from beyond the congregation who lives in the community. You might also consider using e-mail to involve the input of others, perhaps from around the globe. When this group meets, your only task is to promote a lively discussion of the preaching text in relation to their lives and the larger world. Most of all, *listen* actively: draw out responses, insights, issues, correlations, stories, arguments. If possible, provoke *testimonial speech* about God and Christ witnessed to by the text. Take careful notes about what you hear for your preaching.

If you can get your sermon roundtable to go with you, leave the church building from time to time and listen for the gospel in a different context entirely: at the mall, the prison, the homeless shelter, or in the apartments or homes of members of your roundtable group. Shifting the social and cultural location in which the gospel is listened into speech can dramatically change what you wind up preaching each week; it also has the effect of situating your preaching more deeply in the social context around you.

Seek reality. Whereas "relevance" means that you're trying to relate the gospel to life in broad strokes, seeking *reality* in preaching implies that you listen for the ways that those around you *are actually experiencing and interpreting life today in light of the meaning and power of the gospel.* This is another good reason for holding sermon roundtables. If you listen carefully as those around you interact with the biblical text and one another, you can begin to hear the reality (and unreality) that the Word has in their lives. You will hear the gospel being identified and lifted into speech in unique and multiple ways, or avoided and distorted in ways that are often completely unexpected. This will help you think about the gospel in all of its *particularity*, rather than in broad generalities. Ask yourself these questions: Where is the gospel in *this* world, *this* town, *this* congregation, *this* experience, *this* person, *this* place and situation, and at *this* time?

Think "relationship." Although many forms of authority are at work in preaching (biblical authority, the authority of office or ordination, the authority of charisma, the authority of celebrity, etc.), perhaps the most profound and sought-after form of authority in today's context of technology and consumerism is *relational authority*: authority built through trustworthy relationships. Some homileticians have recognized this hunger and encourage preachers to "construct" relationship through increased self-disclosure, changes in dress, conversational styles, and so on.

I believe that roundtable preaching, even in very large church contexts, presents a better and more honest way to develop a deeper relationship in preaching. Roundtable-based preaching embeds preaching in the context of real (not contrived or rhetorically constructed) relationships. If the congregation knows that the preacher's sermons are responding directly to their lives and incorporating their testimonies, this can go a long way toward answering some of the key relational questions that stand in the way of the success of preaching in today's context: Is this someone who wants the gospel to connect with the realities of our lives? That is, is the message real, and will it make a real difference? Is this someone we trust? That is, is the message trustworthy, and does it connect with the core values of this community even as it seeks change? Is this someone who cares about us and the world we experience together? That is, is the message, no matter how hard it may be to hear, ultimately *for* us and the world in which we actually live? Is this someone who will challenge us where we are, in *every* respect? That is, is the message merely a "one tune" song, or can it move with us and grow with us?

Avoid avoidance. Despite what many think, congregations have a deep desire to hear preachers speak about difficult and often divisive theological, ethical, personal, and prophetic issues. Preachers who have done roundtable-based preaching for any length of time tell me that their newly empowered listeners hold their feet to the fire and will not let them avoid dealing with difficult issues: divorce, violence, capital punishment, abortion, suicide, death and dying, lust, greed, injustice, and so on. And listeners empowered as proclaimers hate it when preachers merely give them what they think they want to hear. They expect to be challenged. My advice, then, is not to avoid it when laity in sermon roundtables turn the discussion toward the difficult issues that confront us as individuals, communities, and a nation. Learn from laity what troubles them most about these issues or concerns. Allow them to help you understand how it is that these issues really influence their daily lives and Christian calling. The goal is not to preach what they may want to hear, but to engage the subject in a way that *can be heard and trusted*, because it engages the complexity of these issues and recognizes the real struggles people experience when trying to understand these issues and act as Christians.

Honor complexity. Working closely with laity in sermon brainstorming will make one fact exceedingly clear: life and theology are both filled with gray areas and complexity. Although there are certainly occasions in which the gospel presents us with clear either/or situations, especially when it comes to issues of justice for those who are oppressed, in the great majority of circumstances in life and in theology, there are very few ideas that are cut and dried. For this reason, I generally advise preachers to pay attention to the things they most want to affirm and most want to reject. Whenever you find yourself wanting to shout an ecstatic "yes" to something, ask yourself, "Where is the 'no' in this?" And whenever you find yourself grumbling a frowning "no" to something, stop and ask yourself, "Where is the 'yes' in this?" In most cases this simple practice will help you discover when you are oversimplifying an idea or category that needs to be rendered with more color, texture, and complexity that reflects the true ambiguity of the subject. Pursue these hidden "nos" and "yeses" in your conversations with laity and in your sermons, and you will find that your listeners will be more willing to follow your lead on most issues.

Be generous and forthcoming. Allow for the authentic faith of those you believe are wrong in their understanding of that faith. Although you may be in utterly fundamental disagreement with other Christians, it is important to remember that those with whom you disagree are, in fact, Christians. You can allow for and acknowledge disagreements, and assert an alternative Christian vision without questioning another person's faith. This, I realize, can be extremely difficult at times, especially in circumstances where your own witness or faith itself has been challenged by someone else. In the end, however, it will be far easier for other persons to accept that they have been living out the Christian faith in a way that is wrongheaded, rather than accepting that their entire faith has been a lie.

I also encourage you to be forthcoming. In humility and without implying personal heroism, rehearse your own struggle or process of change. In most instances, you did not arrive full-blown at your current position on an issue. It is likely that you also went through a difficult personal paradigm shift to arrive where you are. Bill Coffin, the great social activist preacher, often took the time to recall bits and pieces of his own struggle around various issues. Coffin would speak candidly about experiences or encounters that had inched him along in his faith and practice. These testimonial moments invariably opened up space in the room for others to consider both the difficulty they were having and the possibility for change.

In the advice I have offered in this chapter, I am urging you to trust the way that God is at work in the lives of the people in your congregation. By encouraging collaborative preaching, my goal is a deeper, more immediate, particular, and focused prophetic engagement within your actual parish context. Much more could be said about the ways in which collaborative preaching works—to empower laity as biblical interpreters, open up new forms of pastoral preaching, change the leadership ethos of a congregation, and more—but you will learn all of that as you go. The point now is to get your first small group together and to start realizing that, other than God, the Bible, and your seminary education, your most important homiletical resource may in fact be your congregation!

19

Homiletical Proverbs

ALYCE M. MCKENZIE

For much of the past fifteen years I've been thinking and writing about how to preach and teach the Bible's Wisdom literature to today's teachers and preachers. Much of that literature is proverbial in form. Study it long enough and you start thinking in proverbs. Recently I told one of my young adult children that "cream doesn't rise to the top unless it learns to swim." Since I made this up, it is an aphorism rather than a proverb, but I don't think the recipient cared which one it was. In fact, I am getting the distinct feeling that my family and the friends I have left are fed up with my quoting proverbs to them. So when the opportunity to write about my best advice on preaching came up, I thought, "What an honor!" And then I thought, "What an outlet!"

My "good advice" remarks will take the form of a series of homiletical proverbs, some of my own coinage, some from the Bible, and some borrowed from valued mentors and colleagues.

The Word Interprets Us

We preach to ourselves, but not to ourselves alone. We come to text and pulpit on behalf of others. Thomas Long, in his book *The Witness of Preaching*, reminds us that "the preacher comes to the pulpit from

114

the pew," fresh from engagement with the community of faith.[1] We discover what to say in Christian preaching as some aspect of our experience in our congregational context creates sparks with some aspect of the text in its context.

I've always felt anxious when a preacher prays before sitting down to study or standing up to preach, "Help me to get out of the way, Lord." I feel anxious because I realize that I myself have nowhere to go. I have no choice but to bring my whole self to the whole text, not just its ideas or its historical background, but its images, its plot, its poetry, its desire not just to say something but do something. I have nowhere else to go but to bring my world to that of the text. In light of that reminder, a better piece of proverbial advice would be "Help me to get in the way of your Holy Spirit so I can be shown a way."

When I "get in the way," I bring my questions and those of my community to the text to be answered, but I also bring answers to the text to be questioned. This is expressed in memorable, proverbial terms by the title of a homiletics textbook from a bygone era, *The Word Interprets Us*.[2] The Word seeks to interpret the uniqueness of each of "us." We need to put ourselves smack dab in the Spirit's way to be claimed and questioned. I quote God's words to the young King Solomon from 1 Kings 3:12 in the first session of my introduction to preaching classes: "No one like you has ever been before you, and no one like you shall arise after you."

No Fear, No Revere

We cherish and nurture our unique expression of God's Word to God's people by habits of prayer, study, and attentiveness. Linda Clader, in her book, *Voicing the Vision*, offers this helpful, proverbially phrased reminder: "Maybe it is not only ethically responsible to practice what you preach." Maybe it is just as important to preach what we practice, to look to the way we allow the Spirit to "guide, enliven, and give meaning" to "our . . . entirely ordinary human lives."[3]

So the question becomes "What do we practice?" The first thing I think we should practice is "the fear of the Lord." "The fear of the LORD is the beginning of knowledge" (Prov. 1:7), the sages of Israel tell us. They tell us it also leads to wisdom (9:10), joy (3:7–8; 15:23;

28:14), and peace (29:25). Says Proverbs 29:25, "The fear of others lays a snare, but the one who trusts in the LORD is secure."

By telling us it is the beginning of knowledge, they mean that this posture before God ought to be both first in importance and first in our sequence of actions. Many students over the years, while growing in confidence and joy in their preaching ministries, have also expressed distress at their abiding uneasiness when faced with the task of preaching. They have asked, "Why haven't I gotten over this by now?" and "Is this a sign of lack of faith on my part?" I assure them that it is not something we should ever "get over." I suggest that they view it not as a sign of the absence of faith, but of the presence of the fear of the Lord.

The fear of the Lord in the Hebrew Scriptures is a mingling of awe before the numinous (Isa. 6), determined loyalty to God and God alone (Deuteronomy), and the conviction that God is the source of all valid guidance in the living of our days (Proverbs). All these postures are responses to the prior grace of God. In the New Testament, Jesus himself as "wisdom in person," invites us to envision fear as faith in his identity and teachings, but the same elements of reverence, loyalty, and following hold true. I can't think of a better posture with which to approach the vocation of preaching than the fear of the Lord. It implies awe and the expectation of being changed and being an agent of change for others. So I've coined this proverb in my teaching: "No fear, no revere."

There Is No Such Thing as Practice Preaching

This mingling of awe and expectation reminds me of the little sign on the preaching lab window at Duke when I was an MDiv student in the late 1970s that read, "There is no such thing as practice preaching!" I think the sign was meant to remind novice preachers that the stakes are higher than we might have thought and that we'd better rely on both preparation and faith. With regard to the need for preparation, a quote John Wesley attributed to St. Augustine comes to mind: "He that made us without ourselves will not save us without ourselves."[4] John Wesley's ministry was built on the conviction that God equips those whom God calls. Paul Scott Wilson insists that "preaching is an event of encounter with God."[5] Remembering that there is no such thing as practice preaching, we stand to preach, filled with the fear of the Lord, that is to say, purged of both panic and pride.

This attitude of humble confidence needs to be nurtured by daily prayer. I have been helped by James Fenhagen's eloquent statement that "the Spirit . . . pulls us inward to listen and pushes us outward . . . with a renewed capacity to love."[6] There can be no authentic ministry without prayer. Fred Craddock reminds us that "a minister's life does not consist in the abundance of words spoken."[7] My version of that thought is a proverb: "If you don't have a prayer life outside the pulpit, you don't have a prayer in the pulpit." Preachers need to read the Bible beyond the utilitarian purpose of "getting up a sermon," with a daily practice of biblical meditation.

The Hearing Ear and the Seeing Eye— the LORD Has Made Them Both

Remembering that we inevitably preach what we practice, I commend attentiveness as the key habit of the preacher, with regard to exegesis of our inward lives, our congregation and community, as well as the biblical text. Barbara Brown Taylor, in her book *The Preaching Life*, calls it being a "detective of divinity."[8] Thomas Troeger challenges preachers with the insight that "it takes discipline to see and to hear the visions and voices of God in our life, discipline every bit as strenuous as exegesis."[9] God praised Solomon because when he asked the young king what he wanted of all the riches of the world, he asked for a "discerning mind," or a "listening heart." He asked to be attentive to what God was doing in all the complex scenarios that awaited his judgment. The sages of Israel valued attentiveness so highly that they regarded it as a gift from God. "The hearing ear and the seeing eye—the LORD has made them both" (Prov. 20:12).

What we discover to say and how we develop it will depend upon the answer to this question: To what are we being attentive? If we are attentive only to questions of authorship and original audience, we will offer a biblical lecture. If we are attentive only to questions about the meaning of words in the text, and the text's literary features and context, we will offer a literary lecture. If we are attentive only to our own desires, needs, and problems, we will deliver a motivational talk. The preacher needs to be attentive to what lies behind the text, in the text, and in front of the text. Every exegetical process and its resultant sermon should show evidence that the preacher has been attentive to all three realms.

Start Your Morning with Morning Pages

In paying attention to the world in front of the text, I recommend the discipline of daily journaling. The Puritans were great proponents of journaling, probably as a result of having gotten rid of the sacrament of confession. It is also a strategy suggested by a number of contemporary writers in literature and religion for unstopping the creativity dam. Julia Cameron, author of *The Artist's Way* and a creativity expert, recommends filling three full sheets of paper each morning. She calls them "morning pages" and suggests we write with honesty and freedom in longhand without stopping to craft or censor our words.[10] When I do this every morning, I am always amazed by how quickly and clearly I can focus and how freely I can write when it comes time for sermon preparation.

Bring All Five Senses to the Text

With regard to the preacher's attentiveness to the world of the text, perhaps the most helpful proverbial advice is Henry Mitchell's from his book *Celebration and Experience in Preaching*. He urges preachers to preach in a way that addresses the totality of the human being, which the preacher can only do when he or she "brings all five senses to the text." That involves being attentive to the whole sensory world of the text, not just its ideas.[11] Notice what genre the text is. Texts want to do things, not just say things.

Don't Spray Windex on the Glass We See in But Darkly

With regard to the world behind the text, be attentive both to what you can and to what you cannot know about the original author and setting. While we cannot recover the exhaustive and precise intention of the author, historical detective work helps us to make educated guesses that inform how the text's message impacts our congregation today. Don't try to answer unanswerable questions for your people. The gaps belong to them too, not just to you. Don't try forcibly to raise the curtain of mystery, or spray Windex on a glass we now see in but darkly. Notice similarities between then and now that make us realize how things haven't changed. Notice differences that make us realize that there is an inseparable distance between us and the world of the text. Explore words and concepts that had different meanings then than they do now.

Do your homework, but when it comes time for sermon making, don't preach your homework. Don't let it go to waste either. Wherever your historical and linguistic homework helps convey the good news, use it. The deeper you delve into the text in its literary, historical, and social contexts, the closer you will connect with your congregation. Augustine's advice in *On Christian Doctrine* was that the purpose of preaching was to teach, delight, and persuade.[12] With the simultaneous existence of biblical illiteracy and biblical hunger in many people's lives, now is a time for teaching.

You Can't Bore the Hell Out of People

To paraphrase Augustine, remember that you can't bore the hell out of people. Give the listener something to do throughout the sermon. You do not have to gain your congregation's attention in the introduction—you have it. It is your job to hold it. Don't follow the same sermon form every week, whatever it is. Have a repertoire of sermon forms that gain and hold attention and shape faith. Avoid the temptation to spill the beans, count the beans, and gather up the beans. Don't explain and overexplain things near the end of the sermon that you have already equipped listeners to figure out for themselves. A sermon only needs one ending. Multiple endings annoy people. Be concrete and specific. As Barbara Brown Taylor points out, "The Incarnate Word preached an incarnate word."[13] Follow Jesus' example and allow abstract concepts to grow out of imagery, story, and metaphor, rather than reducing imagery, story, and metaphor to the role of illustrating concepts. This is in keeping with the way human beings learn and process what we already know.

Make Your Sermons Easy to Say and Hard to Forget

Don't write academic essays for the reading eye with lots of abstract language and qualifying phrases and then try to "memorize them" and wonder why they are so hard to memorize and why you are so afraid that you will lose your train of thought. I advise preachers to prepare their sermon manuscripts as a sequence of scenes, each with a name.

This serves not to "dumb down" the conceptual, theological content of a sermon, but to make it more vivid and memorable. If material is hard to memorize, it probably is because it is not memorable. Ask yourself, "How can I make this memorable?" Remember that the paragraph is not a unit of oral communication but rather of literary communication. Ask yourself, "How can I make this easy to say and hard to forget?"

While many more homiletical proverbs come to mind, I will now cease and desist, reminding myself of the Vermont proverb "Talk less, say more."

Notes

1. Thomas G. Long, *The Witness of Preaching* (Louisville, KY: Westminster John Knox Press, 2005), 3.
2. Merrill Abbey, *The Word Interprets Us* (Nashville: Abingdon Press, 1967).
3. Linda L. Clader, *Voicing the Vision: Imagination and Prophetic Preaching* (Harrisburg, PA: Morehouse Publishing, 2003), 34.
4. John Wesley, "On Working Out Our Own Salvation," in *The Works of John Wesley*, ed. Albert C. Outler (Nashville: Abingdon Press, 1986), vol. 3, 208.
5. Paul Scott Wilson, *The Practice of Preaching, Revised Edition* (Nashville: Abingdon Press, 2nd edition, 2007), 31.
6. James C. Fenhagen, *More Than Wanderers: Spiritual Disciplines for Christian Ministry* (New York: Seabury Press, 1978), 25.
7. Fred B. Craddock, *Preaching* (Nashville: Abingdon Press, 1985), 55.
8. Barbara Brown Taylor, *The Preaching Life* (Cambridge, MA: Cowley Publications, 1993), 50.
9. Thomas H. Troeger, *Creating Fresh Images for Preaching: New Rungs for Jacob's Ladder* (Valley Forge, PA: Judson Press, 1982), 12.
10. See Julia Cameron, *The Artist's Way: A Spiritual Path to Higher Creativity* (New York: Tarcher, 2002), and Julia Cameron, *The Right to Write: An Invitation and Initiation into the Writing Life* (New York: Penguin/Putnam, 1998).
11. Henry H. Mitchell, *Celebration and Experience in Preaching* (Nashville: Abingdon Press, 1990), 17.
12. Saint Augustine, *On Christian Doctrine*, trans. D. W. Robertson Jr., Library of Liberal Arts (New York: Macmillan, 1989), 136.
13. Barbara Brown Taylor, "Preaching the Body," in *Listening to the Word: Studies in Honor of Fred B. Craddock*, ed. Gail R. O'Day and Thomas G. Long (Nashville: Abingdon Press, 1993), 212.

20

To Keep My Head Clear

EARL PALMER

A paraphrase of one of my favorite quotations from Blaise Pascal's *Pensées* goes: "Do great things as though they are small because of Jesus Christ. Do small things as though they are great because of Jesus Christ."[1] I actually carved this inscription on a piece of Puget Sound driftwood that now sits in my office at the church to help keep my head clear. This marker influences me in two ways. First, I am encouraged by what Pascal wrote as if it were for me; second, the marker reminds me to be sure I read the book he wrote and other books too where I will find even more encouraging thoughts.

Pascal is saying that because of Jesus Christ the large matters of life can be handled incrementally, part by part, small step by small step, as though they are small when they are compared to the sheer size of the Lord of life and truth. This "because of Jesus Christ" discovery makes all the difference in charting the course of our lives and our ministries not only in their early months but throughout the whole journey. It teaches me to divide the large questions into their parts and take them on in single steps. It is also a major influence upon my preaching goals. It encourages me to take the time to share the truth of the gospel so that each sermon is sensitive to the small, single steps that add together to become the larger whole.

"Do small things. . . ." This truth is also liberating and upgrades the daily ordinary encounters of life and living. It is an alert to pastors that the work crew at a church conference may in fact be the most important people there from a strategic point of view. They are the ones you get to know the best, just like the everyday lay volunteers whom you know in an ordinary way. These creators of the small parts of the whole may in the end be the most decisive creators of healthy and lasting change. The ways that we as pastors treat the ones we work with has more permanent import for the kingdom than most of our public appearances and larger statements.

I wondered where Pascal came up with this thought, and then I realized that he borrowed it from the final words of St. Paul in his letter to the Philippians. Paul thanks his friends at Philippi for their help to him while he was imprisoned in Rome. They had sent a young man named Epaphroditus to help him and when Epaphroditus became ill, Paul sent him home to Philippi with a truly remarkable letter. Listen to what he says when he thanks them:

> I have learned, in whatever state I am, to be content. I know how to be abased, and I know how to abound; in any and all circumstances I have learned the secret of facing plenty and hunger, abundance and want. I can do all things in him who strengthens me. (Phil. 4:11b–14)

There is a great things—small things mixture here. Paul is saying that he can take in stride on the one side abundance (great things) and, on the other side, want (small things), because of Jesus Christ, who is his friend, his Lord, his Savior, and who is nearby (4:5).

But Paul includes harsher contrasts too—to be abased in defeats and to be honored by success. He can take these large/small contrasts in stride too. He says that he has learned the secret of how to make use of his advantages to the benefit of the ambassadorship mandate he has joined. But he also makes use of his disadvantages, even his persecutions, to the benefit of the same ambassadorship mandate. Can Paul's secret become ours as well? What are your disadvantages and advantages? For Paul there are several: his Roman citizenship helps him, his language skill results in brilliant and totally communicative letters, the wealth of his family and his family connections helped to rescue him from a gang of marauders who wanted to ambush him and kill him. His sister was able to inform a Roman tribune at Jerusalem (Acts 23), who then rescued Paul from the gang of forty plotters. Also, Paul has the ability to make friends. He was a likeable man whom a centurion named Julius respected so much that in a shipwreck near Malta he saved Paul's life (Acts 27). Slaves and fellow prisoners and even guards called him their friend.

Paul also made use of his disadvantages. Imprisonments gave him the chance to write letters and share his faith with other prisoners and their guards too (Phil. 1:13). At Ephesus he could only rent Tyrannus Hall from 3 p.m. to 5 p.m. each day, which seems unfortunate in the heat of the summers at Ephesus, but this happened to be the time slaves could get off work to come and hear Paul. Even this disadvantage became an asset for the ambassadorship of Paul.

I've been thinking about my own experiences in ministry here in Seattle, and I believe the natural advantages have helped me, such as the location of the church building, which is across the street from a major university. But there have also been disadvantages that have made for wonderful surprises. Our sanctuary at University Presbyterian Church is limited to twelve hundred people, which has required that we offer five worship services each Sunday. These have enabled our church to greatly expand ministries of music and Christian education opportunities, for example. The several times of worship each Sunday have become the incentive for creative innovation. For me as a preacher, preaching the same sermon five times has been positive too. I gather momentum as the day goes on.

As you begin your ministry and I continue my ministry, let Blaise Pascal's words ring in our ears: "Do great things as though they are small because of Jesus Christ. Do small things as though they are great because of Jesus Christ." But it takes a clear head to keep track of the great and the small. It takes a mind alive to find time to read a book like the *Pensées*.

I will never forget my Princeton Seminary senior class dinner. The speaker was George Buttrick, then the pastor of Madison Avenue Presbyterian Church in New York City. He challenged our graduating class of future pastors in two directions. First, he urged us to be with our people so that we would become pastors who understood thoughts and feelings of people where they lived and walked so that our ministries would be culturally fluent. But his second counsel seemed to contradict the first: "When you have been on Coney Island, don't tell the people of the concessions on the boardwalk, about which they know. Tell them of the mystery of the sea, about which they know not." He went on: "Don't read only what your people are reading. Read what your people are not reading."

Buttrick impressed upon us the importance of cultivating a mind that is alive. He was making the case for wholeness. In addition to being physically well and spiritually committed, we need to be intellectually alive and healthy. If we're to be effective Christian pastors in the world, we need to learn "the mystery of the sea." There are many ways to keep the mind alive, but I think Buttrick was right to emphasize reading. The desire to read raises questions, however. First, how can I find time to read about the mystery of the sea when I have so many important responsibilities, large and small, among the boardwalk concessions? Second, when I've found time, what should I read?

Each of us as pastors has been given the gift of time and the privilege of organizing it. We each have twenty-four hours a day to own and steward, with more freedom to organize our day and our week than is possible in most professions. But this gift of time has some snares, especially when we allow the hours of the week to confuse themselves into a random jumble of low-quality segments.

The first challenge confronting the pastor who wants to study and read seriously is to develop a philosophy of the week. What is the key to a healthy week? I have a one-word answer: rhythm. To have quality time for my family, for spiritual formation, work, reading, ministry to people, writing, and recreation, I need a rhythmic week. It means that I should think of my life primarily in terms of seven-day periods rather than years, months, or days. It is no mistake that the seven-day week is the biblical yardstick for life measurement. "Six days thou shalt work, and one day thou shalt rest." It is a rhythmic week that the fourth commandment describes.

Furthermore, I can survive high-intensity demands if there is also opportunity for a respite from those demands. And I'll enjoy my rest if it follows real work. The rhythmic contrasts such as fast-slow, many-few, rich-lean, exterior-interior, and time to keep the body healthy–time to keep the mind alive are necessary and make all the difference.

For the second question—What shall I read?—the rhythm principle also applies. I want to read intensively and extensively, light and heavy, great and small, prose and poetry, theology and geology, the Bible and books about the Bible. I want to read and be read to. While electronic media, TV, and film play an increasingly influential part in human communication, they can't replace books. When it comes to imagination, building within that greatest of all collectors of dreams and ideas— the human mind—there is still nothing to match a book read aloud.

In *The Silver Chair*, C. S. Lewis describes Jill's encounter with the lion Aslan: "The voice was not like a man's. It was deeper, wilder, and stronger; a sort of heavy, golden voice. It did not make her any less frightened than she had been before, but it made her frightened in rather a different way."[2] No television or computer screen could capture the vast features of that golden lion quite so wonderfully as the human imagination set in motion by Lewis's words. My advice to young theologians is that you find authors with whom you develop a special sort of friendship. Try to read everything they have written. They aren't masters of our minds, because we won't always agree with what they have written; they're more like companions who especially challenge and encourage our pilgrimage as Christians. They become our mentors.

I'll share my list with you. After the Bible, the following books and authors have had the most influence in my own intellectual and spiritual journey:

- *Pensées* by Blaise Pascal. The most mentally alive writer I know of.
- *Institutes of the Christian Religion* by John Calvin. An impressive and exciting grasp of the large outline of the gospel's meaning.
- *Lectures on Romans* by Martin Luther. As fresh today as in the sixteenth century.
- Karl Barth. Begin with *Dogmatics in Outline*. I deeply appreciate his wholeness and his serious intention to really hear the biblical text. He is the theologians' theologian.
- Dietrich Bonhoeffer. Begin with *Letters and Papers from Prison*. He called out to me to decide, once and for all, about what matters the most in my life.
- C. S. Lewis. Begin with *The Chronicles of Narnia*. I owe so much to Lewis, especially the wonderful mixture of good surprise added to his marvelous skill at description.

- *The Lord of the Rings* by J. R. R. Tolkien. How can anyone miss out on the journey of Frodo and Sam Gamgee?
- G. K. Chesterton. Begin with *Orthodoxy*. I love his humor and ability to stir up my own imagination.
- *Christian Letters to a Post-Christian Age* by Dorothy Sayers is brilliant and earthy.
- Helmut Thielicke. Begin with *How the World Began*. I learned about preaching from Thielicke.
- Leo Tolstoy, Fyodor Dostoevsky, Boris Pasternak, Alexander Solzhenitsyn. These writers have stirred me emotionally and spiritually more than all other novelists.
- T. S. Eliot, W. H. Auden, Robert Frost. These poets have given me a deep respect for words.
- Mark Twain and Robert Benchley have mastered off-the-wall humor with unique insight into personality.
- Paul Tournier possesses psychological wisdom and even-handedness. Try to find his book *Secrets*.

The best books I've read are these:

- My favorite novels are *Crime and Punishment* by Fyodor Dostoevsky, *Les Miserables* by Victor Hugo, and *Huckleberry Finn* by Mark Twain.
- The most impressive recent novels are *The Winds of War* by Herman Wouk and *Peace Like a River* by Leif Enger.
- The most helpful book about the Christian faith is Barth's *Dogmatics in Outline*.
- The most persuasive case for the Christian life is C. S. Lewis's *Screwtape Letters*.
- The most impressive biographies are *Karl Barth* by Eberhard Busch and *William Borden* by Mrs. Howard Taylor.

Notes

1. Blaise Pascal, *Pensées*, trans. A. J. Krailsheimer (Baltimore: Penguin Books, 1968), 316. Here's the entire quotation: "Do small things as if they were great, because of the majesty of Christ, who does them in us and lives our life, and great things as if they were small and easy, because of his almighty power."
2. C. S. Lewis, *The Silver Chair* (New York: Macmillan, 1953), 16.

21

Embracing the Church God Gave Me

EUGENE PETERSON

W hat I most want to tell my colleagues in pastoral work is how I came to reject American illusions and distortions of church and embrace the church God gave me. Church is the textured context—people and place, insiders and outsiders, music and sermons, everything local and relational embedded in Scripture and tradition—in which we grow up in Christ to maturity. But church is difficult. Many Christians find church to be the most difficult aspect of being a Christian. Many drop out. It is no easier for pastors. The attrition rate among pastors leaving their congregations is alarming.

So why church? The short answer is because the Holy Spirit formed it to be a colony of heaven in the country of death, the country that William Blake named, in his comprehensive reimagining of the spiritual life, "land of Ulro." Church is the core element in the strategy of the Holy Spirit for providing human witness and physical presence to the Jesus-inaugurated kingdom of God in this world. It is not that kingdom complete, but it is that kingdom.

My understanding of church as I grew up was of a badly constructed house that had been lived in by renters who didn't keep up with repairs, were sloppy housekeepers, and let crabgrass take over the lawn. Later on after I became a pastor, I assumed that my job was to do major repair work, renovate it from top to bottom, and clean out decades, maybe even centuries, of accumulated debris so that we could make a fresh start.

I acquired this understanding from the pastors that served the congregation I grew up in. They never lasted long in our small Montana town.

One of my favorite sermon texts on church, preached with variations by every pastor I can remember, was from the Song of Songs: "You are beautiful as Tirzah, my love, comely as Jerusalem, terrible as an army with banners" (Song 6:4). The church was the beautiful Tirzah and the army terrible with banners. Those metaphors were filled out with glorious imagery by my pastors. For at least thirty or forty minutes our shabby fixer-upper church with its rotting front porch was transformed into something almost as good as the second coming itself.

Those sermons functioned like the picture on the front of a jigsaw puzzle box. Faced with a thousand disconnected pieces spread out on the table, you keep that picture propped before you. You know that if you just stay at it long enough, all those pieces will finally fit together and make a beautiful picture. But my pastors weren't that patient. Maybe they concluded that there had been some mistake in the packaging of the puzzle and many of the pieces had been accidentally left out. At any rate, it soon became obvious there were not enough pieces in the pews of our congregation to complete the picture of Tirzah and the army terrible with banners. My pastors always left after a couple of years for another congregation. Obviously our church was too far gone in disrepair to spend any more time on it.

Then I became a pastor. I found it hard to abandon my sentimentalized, romantic, crusader illusion of church, an illusion deeply embedded in my imagination. I knew what the church was supposed to look like. My ordination put me in charge of the repairs, renovations, and housekeeping required to bring it up to code so that people could be inspired by the lovely Tirzah and find their disciplined place in the banner-bedecked army.

The illusion dissipated. I soon found that the romantic and crusader imagery that I had grown up with had changed. Sermons from the Song of Songs were no longer preached to eroticize or militarize the church. Bible texts were no longer sufficient for these things. Fresh imagery was now provided by American business. While I was growing up in my out-of-the-way small town, a new generation of pastors had reimagined church. Tirzah and "terrible as an army with banners" had been scrapped and replaced with the imagery of an ecclesiastical business with a mission to market spirituality to consumers and make them happy.

For me, these were new terms for bringing the church's mandate into focus. The church was no longer conceived as something in need of repair but as a business opportunity that would cater to the consumer tastes of spiritually minded sinners both within and without the congregation. It didn't take long for American pastors to find that this worked a lot better as a strategy for whipping the church into shape than the Tirzah and terrible-as-an-army-with-banners sermons. Here were tried-and-true methods developed in the American business world that had an impressive track record of success.

Pastors, I learned, no longer preached fantasy sermons on what the church should be. We could actually do something about the shabby image we had of ourselves. We could use advertising techniques to create an image of church as a place where we and our friends could mix with successful and glamorous people. All we had to do was remove pictures of the God of Gomorrah and Moriah and Golgotha from the walls of our churches and shift things around a bit to make our meeting places more consumer friendly. With God depersonalized and then repackaged as a principle or formula, people could shop at their convenience for whatever sounded or looked as if it would make their lives more interesting and satisfying on their own terms. Marketing research quickly developed to show us just what people wanted in terms of God and religion. As soon as we knew what it was, we gave it to them.

I have been a participating member of the Christian church in North America all my life (seventy-five years at the time I am writing this). For fifty of those years I have had a position of responsibility as pastor in the church. Over the course of these fifty years I have seen both the church and my vocation as a pastor in it relentlessly diminished and corrupted by being redefined in terms of running an ecclesiastical business. The ink on my ordination papers wasn't even dry before I was being told by experts in the field of church that my main task was to run a church after the manner of my brother and sister Christians who run service stations, grocery stores, corporations, banks, hospitals, and financial services. Many of them wrote books and gave lectures on how to do it. I was astonished to learn in one of these best-selling books that the size of my church parking lot had far more to do with how things fared in my congregation than my choice of texts in preaching. After a few years of trying to take all of this seriously, I decided that I was being lied to.

This is the Americanization of congregation. It means turning each congregation into a market for religious consumers, an ecclesiastical business run along the lines of advertising techniques, organizational flow charts, and energized by impressive motivational rhetoric.

The childhood and adolescent illusions I grew up with didn't survive long as I found my way as an adult in the church, worshiping and working for the most part with decidedly unglamorous and often desultory men and women. There were always a few exceptions, but nothing that matched the lissome Tirzah or the terrible army. On the other hand, the pragmatic vocational embrace of American technology and consumerism that promised to rescue congregations from ineffective obscurity violated everything—scriptural, theological, experiential—that formed my identity as a follower of Jesus. It struck me as a terrible desecration of a way of life to which the church had ordained me—something on the order of a vocational abomination of desolation.

And so I set out on a search for "church" that ended me up in Ephesians, which ever since has been my primary text for understanding church—*this* church, the church in which I was a pastor. But I didn't begin with Ephesians. I began with the Acts of the Apostles, in which the term "church" occurs twenty-four times, more times than in any other book in the Bible. It is also the book in which Ephesus is first mentioned.

What I noticed first of all was something that I had never noticed, namely, the exact parallel between the Holy Spirit's conception of Jesus and the Holy Spirit's conception of the church. Luke 1–2 and Acts 1–2 are parallel stories, the birth of our Savior Jesus and the birth of our salvation community.

How did God bring our Savior into our history? We have the story of what he could have done but didn't. God could have sent his son into the world to turn all the stones into bread and solve the hunger problem worldwide. He didn't do it. He could have sent Jesus on tour through Palestine filling in turn the seven grand amphitheaters and hippodromes built by Herod and amazing everyone with supernatural circus performances, impressing the crowds with God in action. He didn't do it. He could have set Jesus up to take over governing the world—no more war, no more injustice, no more crime. He didn't do it.

We also have the story of what he in fact did do. He gave us the miracle of Jesus, but a miracle in the form of a helpless infant born in poverty in a dangerous place with neither understanding nor support from the political, religious, or cultural surroundings. Jesus never left that world he had been born into, that world of vulnerability, marginality, and poverty.

How did God bring our salvation community into the world into our history? Pretty much the same way he brought our Savior into the world—by a miracle, every bit as miraculous as the birth of Jesus, but also under the same conditions as the birth of Jesus. Celebrity was conspicuously absent. Governments were oblivious.

God gave us the miracle of congregation the same way he gave us the miracle of Jesus, by the descent of the dove.[1] The Holy Spirit descended into the womb of Mary in the Galilean village of Nazareth. Thirty or so years later the same Holy Spirit descended into the collective womb of men and women, which included Mary, who had been followers of Jesus. The first conception gave us Jesus, the second conception gave us church.

It was a miracle that didn't look like a miracle—a miracle in the form of the powerless, the vulnerable, the unimportant. It was not so very different from any random congregation we might look up in the yellow pages of our telephone directories. Paul's account of the first-generation church in 1 Corinthians 1:26–29 is totally devoid of the romantic, the glamorous, the celebrity, the influential.

We talk a lot about Christ killed on a cross as a scandal, "a stumbling block to Jews and folly to Gentiles." I want to talk about church, this actual congregation that I attend, as stumbling block, as scandal, as absurd.

The Holy Spirit could have formed congregations out of an elite group of talented men and women who hungered for the "beauty of holiness," congregations as stunning as the curvaceous Tirzah and as terrifying to the forces of evil as the army with banners. Why didn't he? Because that is not the way the Holy Spirit works. We know that is not the way the Savior was brought into our lives. Why would he change strategies in bringing the salvation community, the church, the congregation, into our lives?

Luke is a careful writer. The longer I paid attention to the way Luke told the story of Jesus in the Gospel and saw the parallel to the way he told the story of the church in Acts, I was able to see the same story being lived and told in my congregation. Comprehension came slowly. Those old romantic illusions of sweet Tirzah and the terrible banners were hard to give up. And the deceptive rush of adrenaline and the ego satisfaction that put me in control of a religious business were continuously seductive. Spiritual consumerism, the sin "couching at the door" (Gen. 4:7 KJV) that did Cain in, was always there. But Luke's storytelling had its way with me, and I gradually saw my congregation on his terms. Emily Dickinson has a wonderful line in which she says that "the truth must dazzle gradually or every man go blind."[2]

I realized that this was my place and work in the church, to be a witness to the truth that dazzles gradually. I would be a witness to the Holy Spirit's formation of congregation out of this mixed bag of humanity that is my congregation—broken, hobbled, crippled, sexually abused and spiritually abused, emotionally unstable, passive and passive-aggressive, neurotic men and women; men at fifty who have failed a dozen times and know that they will never amount to anything; women who have been ignored and scorned and abused in a marriage in which they have been faithful; people living with children and spouses deep in addictions; lepers and blind and deaf and dumb sinners; also fresh converts, excited to be in on this new life; spirited young people, energetic and eager to be guided into a life of love and compassion, mission and evangelism; a few seasoned saints who know how to pray and listen and endure; and a considerable number of people who pretty much just show up. I wonder why they bother. There they are: the hot, the cold, and the lukewarm; Christians, half-Christians, almost Christians; New Agers, angry ex-Catholics, sweet new converts. I didn't choose them. I don't *get* to choose them.

Any congregation is adequate for taking a long, loving look at these people. It doesn't seem at all obvious at first, but when we keep at it, persist in this "long, loving look," we realize that we are, in fact, looking at the church, this Holy Spirit–created community that forms

Christ in this place—but not in some rarefied "spiritual" sense, precious souls for whom Christ died. They are that too, but it takes a while to see it, see the various parts of Christ's body here and now: a toe here, a finger there, sagging buttocks and breasts, skinned knees and elbows. Paul's metaphor of the church as members of Christ's body is not a mere metaphor. Metaphors have teeth. They keep us grounded to what is right before us. At the same time they keep us connected to all the operations of the Trinity that we can't see.

Romantic, crusader, and consumer representations of church for too long kept me from recognizing the church right before me and interfered with my participation in the real thing. The church I wanted was the enemy of the church I was given.

Notes

1. See Charles Williams, *The Descent of the Dove: The History of the Holy Sprit in the Church* (London: Longmans, Green & Co., 1939).
2. Emily Dickinson, "Tell all the Truth but tell it slant," in *Collected Poems,* ed. Thomas H. Johnson (Boston: Little, Brown & Co., 1960), 506.

22

Do You Love Me?

HYUNG CHEON RIM

The role of a pastor and preacher is crucial when leading a community of believers. Unless pastors and preachers are spiritually sensitive and alert, they cannot expect their congregations to grow spiritually strong. As a pastor and a preacher leading a Korean American church in the United States, I wrestle with what I need to do in order to become effective in ministry. As I thought about what advice I could give to other pastors and preachers, I decided it would be best to raise some questions and respond with what I have learned during the duration of my ministry.

On Calling: Do You Love the Sheep or Do You Love Jesus?

One of the great lessons for pastors and preachers can be learned from John 21, where the risen Lord appears to Simon Peter by the Sea of Tiberius, and reinstates Peter for ministry. Peter, who, even after witnessing the risen Lord, chose to go out to catch fish, may well have been going through some inner struggles. Perhaps he was struggling with thoughts of disappointment for not being able to keep his word, a sense of shame for denying Jesus, a sense of failure, questions about his uncertain future as a disciple, fear of what others might think of him, and the feeling of incompetence. In ministry, pastors and preachers also experience feelings of disappointment, shame, failure, uncertainty, fear, or sense of incompetence, just like Simon Peter. While it seemed like Peter was lost in the sea of despair, Jesus came to Peter and asked him, "Do you love me?" Jesus then reinstated Peter into ministry by saying, "Feed my sheep." This conversation is very illogical. If Jesus first asked Peter, "Do you love *my sheep*?" and then said, "Feed *my sheep*," it would have been easier to understand. Instead, Jesus said, "Do you love *me*?" and then ordered him, "Feed *my sheep*." This illogical approach, however, provides us with the real meaning of calling and hope when we feel like Simon Peter. This episode reminds us that the centrality of our relationship with Jesus Christ is of the utmost importance for all those who serve in ministry.

Love for the Lord comes before the love for the sheep. Of course it is important to love the sheep, yet if love of the sheep precedes the love for our Savior, every area of ministry will fail because it has become detached from its purpose. If the priority is to love the sheep, then it will be difficult to continue on with the ministry because the sheep are sometimes not easy to love. When the sheep are no longer lovable, pastors may be tempted to give up their role as shepherds. True and lasting ministry comes when a pastor loves the Lord prior to their sheep. The strength of loving the sheep comes from loving the Lord.

On the Word of God: Are You a Speaker or a Listener?

Most people understand the preacher as a person who proclaims and speaks the Word of God, but in actuality preachers are first those who *hear* the Word of God. Those who are called to preach have been commissioned by God to proclaim his message. Unless the preacher has first listened to the Word of God, that person's sermons cannot demonstrate the power of God.

Proclaiming the Word of God without listening to God is what false prophets do. Various techniques can help the preacher develop listening skills. One method is reading and meditating on Scripture like a person eagerly waiting for supper. A second method involves studying the Bible to understand and find the meaning within the given cultural and social context. Another way of listening comes through obedience to the Word. A message that is preached without having the Word of God applied to one's own life is inauthentic and has no power. If a pastor wants to fulfill the role of a preacher, that person must first become an active listener, and then faithfully live a life of obedience to the Word.

On the Work of the Spirit: Relying on Skill or the Spirit

Wisdom gained through prayer and meditation is more precious than any other form of knowledge or skill acquired from educational conferences or seminars. This is not to say that skills and knowledge are unimportant, but yearning for understanding and wisdom without the intervention of the Holy Spirit may not bring needed changes in ministry. In fact, it can even hold people back from experiencing the transformative power of God.

It is important for a preacher to live a life of prayer. I cannot say enough about the importance of spirituality in ministry. Through prayer a preacher breathes. Through a prayerful life, a pastor develops a Christlike heart. One of the great traditions of Korean churches, dating back to 1907, is the *sae-byuck-gi-do* (early morning prayer worship). For most Korean church pastors, each day begins at 5 a.m. or even earlier, and the pastor is required to participate in the early morning prayer worship. A pastor once complained, "Who's the idiot that made this stupid tradition!" One of the church members replied, "Jesus Christ did!" A life of prayer will help us deal with our inner struggles and temptations because, in any given situation, it is important to find the presence of God, trust in the power of the Word, and follow the leading of the Holy Spirit.

On Culture: Blessing or Barrier?

Culture defines how people live, what they think, and what they believe. Unfortunately, culture can become a barrier in the process of understanding the gospel. Pastors and preachers must be sensitive to the issue of understanding and defining a particular culture. I too continuously fight with the problem of culture as a Korean American pastor.

Because Korean culture is rooted in Confucian philosophy, it is especially evident in the social and relational structure. In this system, respect and honor are mostly given to elders and superiors. When

Christianity first came to Korea, Presbyterianism was the best fit, for the concept of *jang-rho* (an elder) was not foreign to Koreans because of the cultural and social structure that already existed within the society. People believed that the leadership of the church should be made up of older adults who have wisdom and life experience. In this postmodern era, Presbyterian denominations in Korea now face new challenges. One major issue is the lack of leadership positions and opportunities for the younger generation, since older generations led and represented the church for decades. A system of church government that was once favored and used to develop and grow churches in Korea has now become somewhat of a barrier and one of the hardest challenges for Korean churches to overcome.

After living in the United States for many years, I have come to realize that the Korean churches have not spent enough time and energy in looking at and evaluating their own cultural issues. The gospel has been enslaved by a culture. Growing up in Korea, I always heard sermons on respecting your parents but never once heard someone preach about not embittering the child. I heard preachers speak about wives needing to be submissive to their husbands, yet rarely heard a preacher say to the husbands that they need to love their wives as Christ loves his church. This is because of a culture under the influence of Confucianism that focuses on respecting the elders and male authority. Even though the Scriptures do not discriminate against age or gender, the church and its preachers are trapped by cultural norms. The growth of the Korean church will not continue unless pastors and preachers are willing to overcome cultural barriers that block their understanding of the gospel.

How should we measure or look at culture? With what criterion should culture be evaluated? We cannot compare one particular culture to Western or American cultural standards, since all cultures have their own limitations. The best way to measure and evaluate culture is through the eyes of our Lord Jesus Christ. For example, Jesus washes the feet of the disciples in John 13 during the Last Supper. Simon Peter refuses to be washed. If one reads this section of Scripture in the context of East Asian culture, it is not Peter who is being defiant or rude, but it is those disciples who allow Jesus to wash their feet. To the eyes of the Asians it is difficult to accept such a situation. It is the young disciples who are receiving the service of their teacher who are being disrespectful. Yet Jesus says, "Unless I wash you, you have no part with me." This demonstrates the depth of Jesus' love, which surpasses the limits of human love. The attitude of Simon Peter, which seems culturally appropriate at the moment, shows the difference between Christ's agape love and human love influenced by relationship and culture.

Pastors and preachers need to work toward understanding and overcoming the problems and barriers associated with our present-day cultures, resist being enslaved or hindered by cultural issues, and let the gospel do its job, for it has the power to transform all cultures.

On the Role of the Preacher: Professional or Prophetic

In our society, pastors are often considered professionals. Theological seminaries, like law schools or medical schools, are categorized as professional graduate schools. So it is natural for others to call those who graduate from seminaries professionals. Yet pastors should not only act as professionals but must also be prophetic preachers.

There are times when preachers will need to proclaim a message from God without compromising or giving in to external concerns. There are times when pastors must lead their sheep through what seems like the valley of the shadow of death, in order finally to lead them to green pasture. Of course there can be risk, struggles, and sufferings when pastors lead their sheep where they cannot see. Yet preachers will fail and the community of believers will suffer if their leaders do not fulfill the duty of showing the people the way of the Lord, regardless of what the world may say.

Prophetic preachers are those who take risks and are ready to sacrifice everything for the sake of proclaiming the Word of God. Jesus said that his disciples must be willing to carry the cross if they want to follow him. If a preacher does not stand in the forefront of carrying the cross, that preacher can never be a good model for others. When interviewing associate pastors, I often hear the question, "What is my job description?" You do not often hear this question in Korea. Not that the job description is unimportant, but it seems ironic since the question often sets boundaries for what a person is willing or not willing to do in ministry. If one's service is based solely on what's on the contract and what's required of the labor laws, how can a person truly expect to carry the cross? How can a pastor be willing to go the distance when he is asked to do so? A seed must die in order to grow and bear fruit. Pastors and preachers must be willing to live a life of a sacrifice that demonstrates the sacrificial nature of pastoral ministry.

On the Attitude for Ministry: Survival or Revival

When I speak with some pastors, I find out that some of them are concerned about playing it safe in their ministry. They do not want to deal with problems and headaches. However, sometimes ministry calls for pastors and preachers who can take the lead and take the needed steps for change. After planting a church and ministering for twelve years, I accepted the call to move my ministry setting to another place. I presently serve one of largest churches in the Korean American community. When I first came on board as senior pastor I prayed, "Lord, should I present the vision you bestowed in me? Or should I wait?" God replied with a very simple question, "Did you come here with a survival mentality?" I answered quietly, "Lord, you know I came here not just to survive." Then God said, "I sent you here for a revival!" This experience helped me to learn that a leader must not have a survival mentality, but that a leader needs to hold to a revival mentality.

Survival mentality focuses on safety and maintaining the status quo, but revival mentality focuses on carrying out the vision and the will of God. Survival mentality focuses on self-preservation; revival mentality focuses on the transformation of others. Survival mentality focuses only on meeting human desires, but revival mentality focuses on what God truly wants. Survival mentality can focus on the negatives and potential threats, but a revival mentality focuses only on the positives and potential benefits. Whatever the ministry context, pastors must maintain a revival mentality, because all are called to do the work of God's kingdom and the transformation that accompanies the reign of God.

23

How to Be an Effective Pastor and Preacher

JOSEPH L. ROBERTS JR.

Suggestions for Pastors Accepting a New Call

During the first few months of a pastorate, study the congregation. It comprises people with different theological orientations and varied educational, experiential, social, and cultural backgrounds. Often some members hold rigid views and may be initially inflexible. Therefore, it is well to approach the congregation carefully, with a listening ear, a discerning eye, and a prayerful disposition.

A new pastor is initially confronted with subtle power plays, prompted by a desire to gain or maintain control over certain aspects of the church's life and mission. There are those who can make large investments of time, energy, and dedication to the church. Often there is nothing wrong with these people or their singular interests, but be on guard. They will try to gain your trust and confidence too early in the game.

Try to discern the strengths and weaknesses of your congregation. Beginning with its strengths, fashion your action plan for ministry and mission; take into account the predominant age group of the active membership of the church.

Survey your geographical surroundings. Visit other churches in the area and seek to know the populations they serve and the ministries they offer. Find out how viable these ministries really are. This information will have a bearing on your direction and the potential for other areas of ministry and service.

But above all, be realistic! It is almost impossible to develop a strong youth ministry in a church and community made up predominantly of older citizens. Deal with this reality positively and celebrate the membership you find.

If you are fortunate enough to have a congregation willing to think "out of the box," some transformative ministries may be possible. For the sake of learning, plan intergenerational activities that will involve your congregation in these transformative ministries, always within the majority's comfort zone. This can easily become an educational, mission experience for the entire congregation.

Special ministries are good for particular populations outside the church's usual sphere of influence if the resources to sponsor them are available. Resources can come through ecumenical relations, community organizations, social agencies, or colleges or universities in your area. These ministries should be initiated on an ad hoc basis, to see if a fit can be found. Don't superimpose them on a congregation where there is no consensus to try them.

Teach, teach, teach during the first two years with a congregation. Review the basic tenets of the denomination, its mission, aim, and ministries with your church officers and congregation. Lead the congregation in meaningful Bible study, which lifts up significant themes in both Old and New Testaments. Additionally, be sure to teach dialogically, in language that can be comfortably understood by all. In other words, "don't pitch the hay so high that the horses can't get to it." Be faithful and consistent as a preacher. Among other very important emphases, seize the moment as an opportunity for theological group therapy.

Suggestions Regarding Making Changes in a New Congregation

It's best to leave most things unchanged in your first year. "If it's not broke, don't fix it." Early on, it's wise to discover the "sacred cows" in the congregation's life. Show some acquaintance with them, whether you are positive or negative about them. Be appreciative but not initially committed to maintain and support these traditions. Indicate that it is too early to make decisions regarding them, that you are still gathering data and testing the waters. Ask for time to understand, deliberate, and pray about them.

However, there are some things that need modification right away. If there is a general consensus in the congregation regarding these things, move decisively (but collaboratively) to make the changes. As you make changes, integrate old ideas with new ones and give the dust time to settle. Don't be too critical of the congregation to which you were called. Remember, it survived all these years without you. If it was not worthy of your ministry, why did you accept the call in the first place?

Suggestions Regarding Making Changes in General

Employ the consensus method of decision making. Listen deeply and carefully in preparation before making changes. Place church officers on all decision-making committees, but be sure to include a larger number of members from the general church population. Encourage all decision makers to enter into the deliberations and speak their minds, following their conscience and experience. Remind them to seek ways to help us glorify God and equip the people for more effective witness and ministry. By making decisions as inclusive as possible, you create more stakeholders, with an investment in the fulfillment of the church's goals.

Identify those members of the congregation who have great influence in the church. They may not be officers, but they greatly influence those who are. Lyle Schaller calls this group "the sub-political structure of the institution." Figure out ways to deal with this structure without becoming captive to it.

Suggestions Regarding Your Conduct as Pastor

1. Love all the members of the congregation, including the unlovable ones.
2. Be open and available to your membership, especially in critical times of personal need.
3. Let members know they can talk with you about anything, but try to avoid allowing them to drop by any time unannounced

just to chat. When possible, encourage them to make an appointment and set starting and ending times for your visits.

4. Celebrate the fact that some members of the congregation have gifts that will be different and superior to yours. Encourage them to use these gifts, and thank God for them.

5. Remember that the pastor is the coach of the team, not always the quarterback. The success of your ministry does not depend on your gifts alone. You are laboring to help all congregants use their gifts to bring in the kingdom of God on earth. By so doing, you make real "the priesthood of all believers."

6. If possible, work to have your congregation be an intergenerational fellowship. By all means, do not favor one age group over another.

7. Roll up your sleeves and work with your people. Don't think more highly of yourself than you ought.

8. Let the congregation know you are vulnerable, but don't use your vulnerability as an excuse for lack of diligence.

9. Recognize that some congregants are gifted in church maintenance (church work), while others are suited for the church's mission (the work of the church). Learn to appreciate and find a place for both groups in the congregation.

10. Realize that some members of your congregation stand in awe of you. Often they are fearful of letting you know their true opinion about a new project or program you endorse. Therefore, be aware that their silence in church meetings does not mean the project has their consent or endorsement. Learn to look and listen and read between the lines.

11. Listen to what people joke about with you. This may be as close as they can comfortably come to making critical suggestions to you. Often what they are joking about needs to be taken very seriously.

12. If there are persons with whom you have disagreements, devise ways to deal with them as soon as possible. Start by thinking through the resources available for conflict resolution in the New Testament. Strive for a win-win resolution, taking some good from all sides of a given issue.

13. Don't block God's light by calling attention to yourself. Don't develop an idolatrous personality cult, centered in your

alleged gifts for ministry. Your gifts are not your own; they are on loan from God, leased to you for use in ministry, for his honor, not yours.

14. Provide a written rationale for major decisions. Have it distributed, reviewed, and studied before a vote is taken. The written report should clearly focus on the benefit of the proposal to the mission of the church. Be open to those who oppose the decision. Let the paper set the parameters for dialogue and resolution of differences.

Suggestions Regarding Preaching

We all have role models, outstanding preachers whose method of preparation and delivery have greatly influenced us. But let us pray that God will help us discover our own preaching voice as soon as possible.

How do we discover this voice? Let's start with these assumptions. The sacred Word is a given, sufficient in and of itself. We preachers merely interpret or unpack it for our congregation in our time. We only discover our own preaching voice when we sense that the sacred Word is being filtered through our personality, in ways that make sparks fly in us. The uniqueness of the preacher comes from the Word's encounter with who we are at a given moment.

Of course, the danger of this approach is pointed out repeatedly. The Word stands as a given, full and complete, but the preacher stands under its judgment and the grace of God, human and fragile. We want a personal dialogue between the Word established and frail messengers like us who attempt to proclaim it. By so doing, we proclaim an authentic, incarnational word in our preaching.

Having stated this perspective, it follows that if we use the lectionary we need to select the passage(s) that resonate with our own spirit at the time. Don't let yourself be forced to deal with the prescribed text if you're just not there at present. Luther taught that the text has to live in us before we can help it live in others. Live with the passage until it lives in you. Read a few chapters preceding the selection for the day as well as one or two beyond. This allows you to connect the dots and discover the nuanced rhythms of the passage. Listen for its music, its harmonies.

Be alert for those words in the passage that leap out at you, insisting on inclusion in the sermon. Be prepared for serendipitous meanings in the passage that can blow you away. At the same time, avoid interpretive excursions. Is what you perceived central to the meaning of the passage? Avoid fanciful exposition even though it is often far more fun.

Remember also the danger of not using the lectionary at all. Without it you may overwork a very narrow set of "favorite texts" and fail to provide the congregation with a balanced diet of rich biblical reflections.

Master the text well enough to be able to recall and "to see" its major thrusts in your mind's eye without referring to the written page of Scripture. Use commentaries for historical and exegetical background, but don't drag your research through the sermon. Commentaries are for our benefit as interpreters of the text. They set the boundaries for us, but the people more often want practical help for everyday living. Read extensively beyond biblical material in classic literature, contemporary religious and theological journals, and secular writings. You will not have the luxury of exhaustive research, but be on the lookout for selections that make the sparks fly in your soul—truths that stop you in your tracks and cause you to utter a deep sigh of wonderful amazement and affirmation.

Bring some order to your research. Jot down major subdivisions that present themselves to you—in other words, create an outline. Try different forms for expressing the truths you encounter. The outline provides pegs that support the sermon and help the congregation stay with you.

Think about your congregation as you ask yourself these next questions. Besides me, who could perhaps be assisted by this message? How best can I help them hear and digest its truths? How can I present it so it can be instructive and healing? Let the images of people in the congregation who might be helped by your message be focused in your preparation.

Now it is time to write out the full manuscript whether you use it in delivery or not. This process will help you present the sermon as your own and begin to internalize it. Read and redraft the manuscript until you are fairly satisfied with it. As you review it, get a general visual sense of where ideas appear on the pages. Remember that it is only a road map, which you may glance at from time to time. Preach from the vision you see. Don't ever let the manuscript control or enslave you. Your manuscript is your friend; it represents the fruit of your extensive preparation for the preaching moment.

Stand under the judgment of the Word yourself. Publicly acknowledge that the message addresses you also. Admit that it strikes a chord in you by confessing that you are also vulnerable and in need of deliverance and healing. Never allow the preaching moment to degenerate into negative diatribe, in which you attempt to "get the people straight."

From time to time it's good to deliver a sermon series on real-life challenges: loneliness, disconnectedness, depression, and emotional challenges such as the struggle of the single parent and the single person, divorced people, betrayal, personal and professional failure, unemployment, strained family relationships, the stages of child development, health problems, sickness, death, and stages in the grieving process.

In preaching, help the congregation understand its solidarity with everyone in God's world, even with our so-called enemies. In preaching, challenge the congregation toward local involvement in its immediate community, encouraging the use of individual gifts to be redemptive wherever we are.

Be an effective pastor and preacher as God's servant to your congregation, and when you have finished you will hear a voice say, "Well done, good and faithful servant!"

24

Love God, Love Your People

MARGUERITE SHUSTER

L ove God, love your people. It's not advice so much as a command of the most uncompromising sort. It's the structure of the Decalogue, the substance of Jesus' summary of the law. Get that right and the rest follows, or if it doesn't follow, what is missing will ultimately show itself to be less than essential. Get that wrong, and in the end, all the achievements apart from it—every spiffy sermon, every leap in the membership rolls—will reveal themselves for the dust that they are.

What kind of encouragement is that? To many of us, such words sound all too much like prescribing a proper diet and exercise for weight loss. However sound the prescription may be, it's hardly news, and the fundamental trouble with it is that we either can't make it work at all, or we can't sustain the effort, or (and here is the hardest part) we don't experience the rewards we expected. Couldn't someone please tell us something *else* to do?

It would hardly do for a seminary professor to imply that the whole enterprise of educating clergy and then publishing articles and chapters and books to try to help them in their ministry is fruitless. As a matter of fact, I think it matters a great deal whether one's doctrine of the Trinity is orthodox, and whether one's sermon is coherently and interestingly designed. Those of us who spend our days working on such matters are not wasting our time. But if one fails to cling to the God whose nature one has so carefully articulated, or if one's engrossing sermon conveys no grace, then the end is worse than the beginning. The danger of all the "something else's" is their tendency to usurp the place of the fundamentals and thus become idols, something of our own construction that we can control much better than God and our neighbor in all their mysterious contrariness.

Some of us, especially when we are young, know too little about the contrariness and hence about the real difficulty of faithful ministry. In the first flush of a call or a conversion experience, love overflows in its emotional as well as its practical aspects. We are ready to go anywhere and serve anyone, at the greatest cost to ourselves. We can hardly imagine either a cooling of the ardor or a lack of striking results for our efforts. But the surer we have been, the more painful the reality that eventually sets in. Sometimes, no doubt, it is to avoid facing the cooling and the less-than-stellar results that we grasp frantically for tools and techniques behind which we can hide. But the more honest we are, the more surely we will suspect, even so, that we have somehow left our first love. What this chapter is really about, then, is not losing our way when the path has become both faint and very steep.

Love God. The feelings do not come easily when expected direction and help seem long delayed, or when disaster has overtaken us in the midst of our most earnest efforts to remain faithful, or when energy is low and hopes have faded. It wasn't supposed to be this way, we are inclined to think. We read and hear about miraculous provision—could the stories be false? We think back to times in our own lives when God's providential care and guidance seemed incontrovertible. Were we deceived? More importantly and more likely, what does it mean if we were not deceived? Unless we have some legitimate reason for supposing otherwise, it does not mean that we have fouled up somehow, and that if only we could get it right (whatever "it" is), all would be well. That's the fundamental mistake engrained in us by our do-it-yourself culture and by all the CEO-style and health-and-wealth paradigms of ministry, those paradigms that teach us that proper procedure on our part will surely produce satisfying results. It is simply a mystery how anyone could read the New Testament, discern the patterns of the lives of the disciples, or contemplate the cross of Jesus Christ and reach any such conclusion. The gospel story is not a tragedy because, and only because, it is finally about God's victory (in a dismaying narrative in which the protagonist has no tragic flaw).

Loving God, then, has everything to do with trusting that victory in the midst of circumstances that look for all the world like defeat. It is not a blind faith; it is confidence, instead, in the resurrection. That confidence then funds—as well as directs and constrains— everything else. But it funds it all as the firstfruits, the sure promise, of the harvest, *not* as if the harvest had already come and the only reason we are not healthy, wealthy, and wise is that we have unaccountably failed to take advantage of it.

Loving God, trusting his final victory, involves taking the whole earthly story in all its brutal messiness seriously, in our living and in our preaching, for the crucifixion was the *necessary* precursor to resurrection—necessary not, perhaps, in some vague theoretical sense, for one can imagine restoration to life provided in the face of a death that came in one's sleep—but necessary to the atoning work of the one who bore in his human body not just our weakness and mortality but our sin. Victories involve real enemies, real battles, and almost inevitably real suffering. How then can we read and proclaim the gospel story by bowdlerizing it, by compiling little pink books of Bible promises that ensure our preaching will be "uplifting"? Not, of course, that the point is to make the opposite error and specialize in the sayings of a little black book of Bible curses. The point is that the whole counsel of God contains all the terror and complexity and failure and defeat, as well as the mysterious joys and gifts, of ordinary human life. If we really trust God, we will trust him right there, and our preaching will not dance daintily around the difficulties. Because if God isn't big enough for difficulties, he isn't big enough, and we will in the end deceive and confuse our people, whose lives don't quite measure up to the idealized pictures we are so tempted to present. We cannot truly love God if we love only carefully "Photoshopped" pictures of him, from which everything marring a harmonious view has been eliminated. If we try, or if we present such a picture to others, it is not God whom we love but some idealized deity of our own design. Even the promise of the abundant life God offers must be presented in the way that God offers it, not as the world defines it.

Besides a sober honesty with ourselves and others about what God has done and the obstacles in the face of which he has done it, loving God also involves a certain self-sacrificial style of discipleship. Face it: love, if it is love, always involves sacrifice. Sometimes the joy of a relationship makes the sacrifice seem like nothing. At other times, commitment to the relationship sustains one in the necessary sacrifices despite sentiments that would lead anywhere or everywhere but where one must go. A longing for holiness is rather out of fashion these days, and if such a reference makes one squirm a bit, I have made my point. No doubt there is an ascetic impulse that can merge all too readily with a self-justifying and destructive masochism; one can surely fall off the trolley on that side. But today, cultural forces are more strongly arrayed to push us off the other side, the side on which every sort of self-indulgence, self-centeredness, and capitulation to the allure of mammon is justified under the rubrics of health, self-care, and celebration of life.

True, certain pastor-search committees today will be populated by those who want a pastor—and a Jesus—whom they can "hang out" with, someone whom they see as being basically just like them and with whom, therefore, they are perfectly comfortable. That's fine so long as one doesn't really need a pastor—or a God. While one understands and affirms such persons' distaste for all the "holier than thou" presentations (and visions) of self that can make pastors simply obnoxious, one fears that the less defensible aspect of the impulse is to have a pastor whose character and preaching will make no actual demands, will lead to no real disturbance of one's lifestyle and commitments. It may betray an underlying spiritual laziness, a refusal even to aspire to anything higher and harder. Capitulating to desires of this sort means in the end choosing to please people rather than seeking to live up to the best that one knows. I suspect that the best that one knows involves a good deal more self-discipline and a good deal more awe before the holy Lord than will ever be exactly popular.

This element of sternness and exclusivity in one's love for God is precisely what enables one actually to love one's people and not simply use them for one's self-aggrandizement. It can free one to keep on loving all those folks whose troubles all the good advice and good cheer in the world will never "fix." Indeed, it may at last teach one that the only help one can give begins when, because one trusts in the Lord's adequacy, one stops needing to "fix" folks. What they need most, of course, is a pastor who is not afraid to stick around even if it doesn't get better, for how can they be expected to find their recalcitrant suffering bearable if even their pastor cannot tolerate it over the long haul?

Such a pastor will not leave the care of his or her people to someone else so that he or she can attend to administrative tasks, as if the mechanics of the institution were more the pastor's job than the human condition of the people. He or she will neither feel the need to beat people up from the pulpit, as if being punitive were the measure of faithfulness, nor be squeamish about the hard word that is sometimes called for. The pastor who loves the people will seek to be an agent of God's grace and mercy, genuinely wishing the people well but not confusing things going well with their being easy. In fact, to love people may often require being willing to say that, given the choice between a route that requires courage and one that offers comfort, the one that requires courage has a certain moral presumption in its favor. It is the easy road that should raise the most suspicions in a broken world like ours. The loving thing is the true one—true not in a wooden and brutal sense, but true before God.

These people whom we commit ourselves to love will surely disappoint us, even as God disappoints so many of our expectations. Sometimes they will disappoint us because they do not make the progress we think they ought. Sometimes they will disappoint us because they do not offer us the appreciation we long for. Sometimes their sorrows will break our hearts. And sometimes we will be ashamed as we find them far more faithful than we are ourselves. But there they are—the painfully mixed and highly particular lot the Lord has given specifically to us, given into our care.

Love God, love your people—honestly, without looking away from the hard parts, without expecting "doing it right" to "work" according to this world's standards. There is, after all, no very sound reason to suppose it will, for apart from the resurrection, the gospel itself could look for all the world like a failure. The great cloud of witnesses of Hebrews 11 all died without having received what was promised. Why? Because God has provided something better (Heb. 11:39–40).

"What no eye has seen, nor ear heard, nor the human heart conceived"—that is "what God has prepared for those who love him" (1 Cor. 2:9). To believe that deeply is to be made wonderfully free to obey and trust the only one who, in the end, can make it all worthwhile no matter what, and thus to be genuinely free to give ourselves to our people.

25

An Old Preacher's Unsolicited Advice

GARDNER TAYLOR

My first piece of advice to preachers is something I learned early on and found confirmed in more than seventy years since first standing in a pulpit and trying to utter the glorious gospel of Jesus Christ. That lesson, so deeply scored into every part of my being, is that no earthly creature will ever give adequate utterance to the "gospel of Jesus Christ."

Every person who preaches uses the poverty of human language to confront and to declare the Word of God, which belongs to a realm in and beyond the verbiage of the world. The tidings of grace contained in what Arthur Gossip called in his day "twenty seven pamphlets" are that and infinitely more. The proof lies in the truth that after two thousand years, the words and assertions of these "pamphlets" are too good to be true, but are also actually true—truer than any conception of truth we may hold. The first incredible assertion that baffles the mind and humbles any preacher's attempt to "make it plain," as black congregations once "talked back" to the preacher, is that "in the beginning was the Word . . ." (John 1:1).

What beginning? The preacher's mind is embarrassed trying to think of some "situation," if that word is applicable, in which there is no "situation." Then the Gospel in this way and that looks back to Genesis at a Sovereign Voice saying again and again, "Let there be . . ."

And out of that Word, uttered some nine times, the glory and splendor of the universe appeared with a tenant in place who would be called "Adam." This was but the first of the highly incredible assertions that of necessity would make any mortal draw back.

The second piece of advice to colleagues about preaching is to warn the woman or man who feels the compulsion of this work that a recurring sense of inadequacy goes with the calling. Every person so positioned would like to feel that all is blithe and cheerful. The sooner the preacher realizes that there is "a stormy north side" to this work, the better. Even the most cursory glance at the lives of some of the better known and remembered preachers shows they have wrestled with, among many other things, hypersensitivity.

Frederick Robertson of Brighton was considered the finest of the English preachers of the nineteenth century. Harry Emerson Fosdick, of blessed memory, said once that Frederick Robertson "primed his pump." Robertson's biographers have said that his make-up was as sensitive as the human eye. There are examples of this in his record. After a sermon in Brighton's Trinity Chapel, a woman complimented the preacher by saying what a marvelous sermon she had just heard. Robertson's replied, "Thank you, Madam, the devil has already told me so."

Who can forget the mammoth preaching influence of Harry Emerson Fosdick, though all who heard him realized that his voice lacked a certain resonance? His years at the Riverside Church represent a high-water mark of American preaching. Many have forgotten, happily, that Fosdick spent months in a mental institution, so high strung was his sensitivity. Discovering his book *The Meaning of Prayer* in Bishop Joseph's residence in South India, I was surprised to learn later that Fosdick once said that without that time of nervous breakdown, he doubted that he would ever have written such a book.

Alexander McClaren belongs easily among the titans of pulpit discourse. Some of us think of McClaren as the unmatched preaching expositor in all of the recent centuries. James Luther Adams once said that he never dealt with a passage that McClaren had dealt with by reading McClaren's exposition first, because if he did, he had to take McClaren's outline or get another text. Yet McClaren's biographies tell us he was so shy he could not even speak to a servant girl in his Manchester apartment about spiritual matters.

McClaren's shyness was repeated in Robert McCracken, the Scot who succeeded Fosdick at Riverside. Anyone who knew him will join my opinion that McCracken was extremely bashful, almost embarrassingly so. American effusiveness would put a blush on his face, reducing him to a stutter. Yet McCracken stood well to the fore in that galaxy of New York preachers that was, perhaps, the greatest concentration of preaching gifts in one city in all of the Christian centuries and that included Sandy Ray and Adam Clayton Powell Jr. One of the most notable in that splendid list of preachers who will remain nameless for obvious reasons once said to me that he had to fight all of his years with a feeling of worthlessness.

Someone will inevitably ask the question as to how the preacher is to manage these demons, grim reminders of our human frailty. These negative afflictions must be offered to God for whatever use it may please him to put them, and the history of preaching offers many examples of how these darkly visaged features of personality might in their own way, or better still, his way, be made to serve the kingdom of Christ Jesus.

Perhaps the classic example is that of the apostle Paul as preacher, a man who found it difficult to find common cause with others. Perhaps the most glaring illustration of Paul's stubbornness was the way he reacted to Barnabas when that benefactor of the great apostle wanted to take John Mark on another missionary journey. Paul objected, though Barnabas had made Paul's acceptance among the Christian community less difficult.

This apparent stubbornness, which seems unattractive in Paul, may have been what made him the apostle and preacher that he was. Had he been less stubborn he may never have led that small company of believers to free themselves from the domination of those who tried to keep Christianity a sect of Judaism rather than a society of the resurrection. We hear him in Galatians tell Christians to "stand fast therefore in the liberty wherewith Christ hath made us free" (Gal. 5:1 KJV).

We know of the conflict of faith and doubt in Mother Teresa who confessed to experiencing what she called "the silent emptiness," which a sixteenth-century mystic, describing the same malady, spoke of as the "dark night of the soul." Might it be that this benefactor of humanity in our day was prodded into her prodigious service to the poor and needy by the spiritual affliction she describes so rivetingly as "emptiness and darkness"? I participate in an "On Faith Panel" sponsored weekly by *Newsweek* magazine and the *Washington Post*. I have suggested there that faith and doubt are two sides of the same coin. One side, held up to the light, reflects brightness while the bottom side is in shadows. Perhaps this protracted spiritual misery lay at the root of Mother Teresa's life of service to "the least of these."

George Buttrick, referring to Thornton Wilder's collection of three-minute plays, once said, "The Angel has just troubled the waters. It is then that they give healing." A cripple who has waited there as many years as the Israelites were in the wilderness moves toward the pool only to find that a "newcomer," a physician with swifter than a cripple's limbs is beating him to the chance. Then the angel bars the physician. He protests, but the angel is adamant. He bids the physician stand back—the healing is not for him. "Without your wound where would your power be?"[1]

The preacher must ever remember her or his limitations. Recognizing the deficits of character and the other problems of life, the preacher will find that these are the very avenues by which she or he will be able to find access to the problems and limitations that others face. The preacher's job then is to make those negatives, something that plagues us all, available for the gospel to be preached. The preacher's weakness is the avenue by which the power of God finds access to human need.

Who is sufficient for these things? There is a strong sense that everyone called to the responsibility of representing God to people and people to God is capable of meeting this crucial issue. Once in a preaching class at Shaw University, I happened to take my thumb and to press it on a desk. I then said that that thumbprint had never been produced before, nor would it ever be seen again. Dean J. T. Roberson at Shaw Divinity School and the Reverend Sherri Graham took this almost casual remark and began examining what they called the DNA of preaching. Now surely if the thumb, almost an appendix of the human person, is unique to every human being, then one can assert with some confidence that the human mind and emotions are also unique. They occur in each preacher as an original, were never seen before in all of human existence, and will never be seen again. Such is the warrant for each preacher to offer the gospel in terms of who she or he is. This ought to remove the temptation to copy other preachers. It ought to give each preacher the sense of her or his worth to the Savior's kingdom.

The Christian pulpit has had more than its share of rare and winsome personalities. Looking back now on the golden age of preaching in New York, the idea of sermonic DNA is clearly evident. In my earlier years in New York, I can remember preachers of incandescent gift. Each one was different, because the homiletical DNA of each was different. My colleague in Brooklyn for thirty-five years was Sandy Ray, pastor of Cornerstone Baptist Church. Ray possessed sheer genius in finding great contemporary messages in biblical passages. He once said that he preached in the right lane because that was the side on which the exit ramps were located on New York parkways. Paul Scherer was pastor of Holy Trinity Lutheran Church and a preacher of vivid imagination. He once said that the hour of worship is that time when we bring the gods we have made before the God who has made us. Robert McCracken at the Riverside Church carried in his preaching and in his soul a kind of wistfulness, plus a Scottish brogue, both of which found their source in the moors and mists of the valleys and hills of his beloved homeland. Adam Clayton Powell Jr., at the Abyssinian Baptist Church, was on fire with a prophet's anger about injustice, a theme that was as natural to him as breathing. People still remember the preaching DNA of George Buttrick, a man who possessed both a relentless logic and the music of a poet. Everyone who preaches brings to the task the totality of his or her personality. The qualities that create the preacher grow out of the mystical interplay of the gospel on the mental and emotional equipment of each preacher. An awareness of this fact gives to each an authenticity and a style to be found nowhere else.

About the length of a sermon I will make two comments. Two Scottish crofters sat together in a highland church. The preacher's sermon seemed to go on interminably. The first farmer said to the second, "When is he going to finish?" The answer came back, "He is finished now, he just won't quit." The preacher does well who cultivates some terminal facility.

I'm also reminded of an Anglican bishop who attended an evening service in the English midlands. When the service was over, the bishop said to the rector, "I thought your sermon to the people this evening was rather brief." The rector replied, "Better to be brief than boring." To which the bishop gave the rejoinder, "But, sir, you were both." My late, great friend Samuel Proctor believed that in the development of the sermon there ought to be a Hegelian process of thesis, antithesis, and synthesis, though one ought not show too severely the skeleton of the sermon. Put some flesh on it!

A sermon is hardly worth preaching that does not appeal to the mind and the heart. James Denny once advised his students, "Preach to me what you believe—I have doubts enough of my own." As to the mind, people who enter church have a right to bring their heads with them. At the same time people are affected by their emotions. The great Southern Baptist preacher George W. Truett had the assignment as a young student of preaching one summer out on what was then the frontier of America. Some laymen told him about a man with the reputation of being stern and somewhat withdrawn from religious life. They urged the young preacher to try to engage this rancher in a religious conversation. So Truett went to the hard-bitten frontiersman's home, where he was welcomed but not with great warmth. When Truett asked the man about his mother, "Was she a Christian?" the stern rancher's face softened immediately as he remembered his childhood. We are all affected by our emotions, and the sermon, without pandering, has every right to speak to that crucial part of every congregant's psyche.

In the same way, the emotions of the congregation are also in the one who stands before them. The task of preaching is itself daunting enough. Few are the preachers who rest easily during weekends. Most congregations are not aware of the sheer tension involved in standing before the people of God seeking to make clear and woo them by words into recognizing the inexpressible honor and burden that belongs to them as sons and daughters of God. Restlessness for the preacher on Saturday night and Sunday morning is almost terrifying. I know that in my own case there was always a gripping dread as the weekend came, mingled with anticipation and eagerness, to be sure, but almost a terror. After nearly seventy years in pulpits in every corner of the world, I testify that it takes longer than that to get over this occupational hazard. It will likely follow you when your weekly task has passed. My doctors, John Cassidy and Leroy Darkes, tell me that this is normal. We live in a coarse time when many preachers seek to appeal to the materialism that so many are willing to substitute for that spiritual hunger everyone experiences. This has led to a kind of preaching in which the great transactions of Scripture are hardly mentioned. The cross of Christ and his resurrection stand at the heart of the gospel as the true clue to the character of God and the value of our humanity. These pivotal emphases of the New Testament are hardly mentioned in so much of our preaching. Here is the true reason for the restlessness of our days and years in the earth.

Armed with these transactions and all of the possibilities that flow from them, the preacher is to do his work in the pulpit and out. It is fidelity to these infinitely crucial events that has made the history of the pulpit glorious. Joseph Fort Newton once wrote about the royal lineage of the pulpit:

> One who has ears can hear the far-off thunder of Savanarola, the deep bass voice of Luther, the fiery speech of Knox—to say nothing of Beecher turning the Plymouth Church Pulpit into an altar for Freedom's call. Men mighty in the spirit, before whom princes trembled. No young person need falter at the steps of the pulpit, consecrated as it is by so much of genius, power and beauty. If the preacher would touch the soul of his or her listeners, enable sorrowing eyes to see majestic meanings in life, and turn the thought of youth from glittering semblance of life to homage for truth, beauty, character, and the service of humanity, let the preaching one enter the pulpit humbly and reverently, in love of God and love of people, speak the truth as God gives him or her to see it in a spirit and form worthy of the truth that is in Christ, and that voice will echo in the hearts of people long after the preacher has fallen asleep.[2]

Newton has spoken well. There are many voices raised in the public square. Our ears are deafened with self-serving counterfeits for the full life. Each one leaves the hearer momentarily satisfied but having no real nourishment, like a child fed a diet of candy when the human body demands food that builds and sustains life.

The preacher who grasps these real and deepest needs of the human spirit will discover that people hungering for nourishment that gives meaning and power to life will happily find strength of soul and the vigor and vision splendid for which we human beings were made and the attainment of which constitutes the point of our existence in the earth. To these things preachers are called, and in service to them one will find a fulfillment beyond comparison. "Let us therefore follow after the things which make for peace, and things wherewith one may edify another" (Rom. 14:19 KJV).

Notes

1. George Buttrick, *God, Pain, and Evil* (Nashville: Abingdon Press, 1966), 195.
2. Joseph Fort Newton, *The New Preaching* (Nashville: Cokesbury, 1930), 45.

26

I Thank You, God, My Heart Is Beating

The Place of Elemental Prayer
in a Preacher's Life

THOMAS H. TROEGER

W hat is your best advice to your colleagues about preaching?" There are two extremes in answering this question. The first is that the advisor will assume that she or he is the universal human being and that what works for her or him should work for all. This approach results in theological tyranny: "I have the answer and here it is!" The second extreme is to answer the question in such vague and general terms that no one can disagree and no one can learn a blessed thing from what is advised.

I aim to avoid both pitfalls by being specific in giving my best advice *to myself* about preaching and then saying, "Okay, if this does not work for you, tell me what it is that works for you." If you hate what I write, it may yet be profoundly helpful to you, providing you take the time to say, "What Troeger advises is no good for me because what I need to do is . . ."

So here comes my best advice to myself, a preacher of forty years' experience who is by the grace of God sometimes, and sometimes not, a vessel of the Spirit, of the living Christ, of a word that is truer and more helpful to others than I personally could ever imagine or accomplish on my own.

I start with morning. Early morning. For I am a morning person. Beginning right here, if your metabolism is different from mine, you

may need to change what I am advising to myself to fit your own bod-
ily rhythms. At any rate, every morning, very early, I arise and go on
a power walk, arms swinging, feet and legs taking big, loping strides.
I always pray the exact same words as I start out:

I thank you, God, my heart is beating.
I thank you my lungs are breathing.
I thank you there is air to breathe
and water to drink and wash with.
I thank you for the love of Jesus Christ,
especially as it is incarnate in my wife, Merle Marie.
I bless you.
I praise you.
I thank you. Amen.

Then I fall silent. Dead silent. I wait upon the Spirit. Of course,
there are ten thousand voices rising in me to pray for other things: my
friend who is ill, the violence that is killing people, a colleague who
needs help, a family member in distress, a church in fragments, and
so forth. But I silence all these voices, not because I lack compassion
or concern, but I realize my order of prayers is the order of my
mind—my puny, limited, biased, inadequate mind. Sometimes I give
the voices names if they won't shut up. I say, "All right, Robert, that's
enough. I must to tend to God now." "Sarah, I know all about it, but
wait your turn. I need to hear God now."

And what do I get for all of this? I see the sun is trying to break
through the clouds. I hear the crows setting up a ruckus on the tall
hickory trees. I note there is a spot of gold light on the field interwo-
ven with dark evergreens. Sometimes I receive much less than this:
nothing. I hear nothing. I see nothing. I note nothing.

But then nothing becomes something, and my words of prayer
come back to me—only they come back bearing the sound of the
crows, the gold of the dawn, and some sense of presence, wonder, an
ineffable depth just beyond the nimbus of dawn light on the treetops
as a word: no! More accurately, they come back as a realization that
is in words but beyond words. "I thank you, God, my heart is beating"
is transfigured into realizing that every tree, every branch, every leaf,
every bird I hear singing, every breath, every pulse beat, every stone

beneath my feet is arising from a reality I had nothing to do in creating, nothing to do in giving shape and color. My own being and the being of the world about me is all a gift. All unearned. All grace. Many mornings I become completely still, other than the swinging of my arms and the stride of my legs. I am stilled by the sheer extravagance of what God has done. Stilled by the privilege of seeing it, hearing it, sensing it. Stilled by joy, by thanksgiving, by the way I no longer assume that I deserve to exist.

"I thank you my lungs are breathing." By now my power walk has me panting. My lungs are working hard. Air is making sound going in and out of me. I am not mind. I am not thought. I am not Reverend Troeger. I am not Professor Troeger. I am bellows. I am air sacks: expanding, contracting, expanding, contracting, expanding, contracting. I am Adam: earth creature, mud creature. God is breathing air into my nostrils. God is with me, filling me with breath, letting breath out of me. I am thankful Adam, thankful earth creature, thankful mud creature. I am in a state of elemental prayer. I am in the same mode of existence as atoms and cells: utterly, absolutely, totally dependent upon the source and core of being for every instant of my being. "It is the Lord who has made us and not we ourselves." The words of the psalmist are no longer mere words. They are bone and cell and muscle and tendon of my skeletal, fleshy being panting amid the trees in the morning air.

"I thank you for the love of Jesus Christ, especially as it is incarnate in my wife, Merle Marie." For a moment theologically sophisticated voices interrupt. "This is heresy, or if not heresy, then shoddy thinking about incarnation. The word became flesh in Christ, in a particular human being, Jesus of Nazareth. Perhaps your wife embodies the love of Christ, but surely she does not incarnate Christ."

I think of Merle Marie holding me when my father died, when my mother died, when my older brother died. I think of her forgiving me when I acted wrongly toward her. I think of her passing me bread and wine at supper at our counter in the kitchen. I think of her lips on mine. I think of Mary wrongly identifying Christ as the gardener, the disciples identifying Christ as a ghost, the disciples on the road to Emmaus thinking him as nothing more than a fellow traveler. I think of the constant failure of Christ's followers to recognize the living Christ in the Gospel accounts of the resurrection, and I pray that I will not be so obtuse. Then I hear the skies and the earth saying to all the nit-picking theological voices, "Hush! The risen Christ is here. Now. In Tom's wife, and in millions of others."

At that command from heaven my heart moves beyond all arguments, all acts of ratiocination to praise, to an outpouring of unmeasurable, unreasonable, unchecked, uncalculated, unstoppable, unimaginable, unspeakable adoration. It is a way of being that flows with the electrical charge of the atoms, with the motions of cellular life, with the choreography of the galaxies, with the music of the creatures, with the drumbeat of the waves, with the drifting of the clouds, with the unheard anthems of the cherubim.

"I bless you.

I praise you.

I thank you. Amen."

I arrive home from my walk—exhausted, exhilarated, resurrected, filled with new life, filled with a sense of the wonder and liveliness of God.

I shower. I dress. I have breakfast with my wife. I hurry off to the office. Somebody cuts in front of me on the highway. Somebody goes through a red light. Somebody is angry I did not answer their e-mail earlier. Somebody needs help. Somebody, somebody, somebody.

But in my heart music keeps sounding: the music of the crows, the music of the early light in the trees, the music of that walk when the morning dawned on God's creation as beautifully as it dawned the first day the sun rose over the horizon of earth. In the music I hear something, I receive something: strength to do the ministry God is calling me to do.

I go home and take out my silver flute, the flute I spent my entire life's savings to buy when I was sixteen years old. I play the Handel sonata in A minor, the one with the long, arching, yearning triplets that breaks my heart in the same way that all the sadness of the day now past breaks my heart. In the vibrations in the air and beneath my fingertips in the silver pipe I sense again the presence I felt on my morning walk: the irrepressible vitalities of the divine resilience, the breath of God, the risen Christ. When I finish, I sit down and read the lessons I must preach on Sunday morning. They are soaked with the waters of the everlasting spring of Christ, but the waters are rising from my soul as well as the text. Elemental prayer has prepared me to prepare to preach.

What has all of this to do with you? What has this to do with giving you my best advice for preaching? Nothing and everything. Nothing because, as I said right at the start, the worst thing about many people who give advice is that they assume that their unique methods and ways of being are universally true. I have not assumed that to be the case in anything I have written here or elsewhere. What I have assumed is that you and I are equally human, equally children of God, bearing God's image and hungering to know the one who has created us. Therefore, I have told you what I do, hoping that you may discover in the specifics of my life what you need for the specifics of your life as a preacher.

You may not need to walk in the morning. You may not need to thank God in the words of the prayer I offer. You may not need to listen to the crows and to mark the morning light in the crowns of the trees. You may not need to have a life partner who is for you the incarnation of Christ anew. You may not need to play a silver flute. But you will need what these represent: You will need elemental prayer, prayer that arises from the very core of who you are, prayer that touches the intersection of heart and mind and soul and strength with the wonder, the glory, the grace, the love of God. You will need to keep alive day by day a vital, creative, ever enlivening relationship to the deep, dear core of things, to the source of every good and perfect gift, to the breath who breathes all things into being, who sets the electrons and the galaxies spinning, who raised Christ from death and sent the wind and fire of the Spirit upon the early church.

You will need elemental prayer. You will need a relationship to God honest enough that you can cry out to God when you feel abandoned, generous enough that you can sing to God when your heart overflows with gratitude, and broad enough that you can harvest the fruits of precise thinking and fervent feeling to give glory to God now and forevermore.

27

Learning and the Life of the Pastor

LEANNE VAN DYK

The life of a congregational minister is varied, challenging, and constantly changing. It is often noted that ministry today is strikingly different than it was a generation ago. The expectations are higher and the demands more numerous. In recent years, several studies have reported that the ministry is hard on the health of the minister. A 2006 study by the Evangelical Lutheran Church in America, for example, cited rates of stress, depression, and addiction dependencies in clergy were across the board higher than in the general population. In a lecture at a 2004 conference in Washington, D.C., on public health and the environment, Bethann Cottrell also documented the high rates of obesity, mental health, heart disease, and stress in clergy. It appears that ministry is a dangerous profession.

The strategies for sustaining pastoral ministry are wide-ranging and include a number of efforts, including maintaining healthy boundaries, exercising, and participating in peer support groups. Another strategy is creating and then pursuing a lifelong learning plan. The rapid pace of change in the ministry and the multiple demands on the pastor mean that the MDiv degree is the entry point, not the finish line, of theological education. A plan for lifelong learning can serve as one tool to encourage, strengthen, and deepen the pastor. Such a plan, especially if supported by the congregation with needed budget and policies, can include continuing education courses and periodic sabbaticals for research and consultation. It should also include a regular pattern of reading. A plan of reading can be an individual exercise, or a small group pattern, or both.

This essay will suggest particular ways that reading in the pastoral life can enrich preaching and pastoral care. Reading both fiction and nonfiction will open up areas of human experience at a level far beyond the pastor's own circle of family, friends, and congregation. In this way, the minister will be able to explore the particularities of people and the nuances of the gospel in ways that will empower preaching and inform pastoral care. Preaching in particular can benefit from reading, both in theological and biblical disciplines, and also in fiction and nonfiction sources. The preacher who reads consistently preaches more creatively and compellingly because resources far beyond the experience of the preacher are brought to the task of proclamation.

One readily accessible source of excellent reading material is the annual Pulitzer Prizes, awarded in journalism, commentary, poetry, fiction, and other literary categories. The Pulitzer Prizes offer a range of options, from brief newspaper commentaries to full-length biographies and fiction. This annual list focuses on current global issues that are explored in the nation's most respected newspapers as well as the best of new fiction and nonfiction. It is only the narrowest slice of what is worthy of reading, but it cannot be surpassed in terms of quality and timeliness.

The Pulitzer Prize winners from 2006 and 2007 provide an example of how reading like this can enrich and sustain ministry. Some of the winners of 2006 include *Washington Post* journalists Susan Schmidt, James Grimaldi, and R. Jeffrey Smit, who investigated the tangled political connections of Jack Abramoff. A story like this, in all its complexities and layers, gives the preacher a vivid case study of sin. Here is a story of astounding deceit and patronage, and blatant brokering of power and influence. Honest preaching on sin must display an awareness of the parasitic character of sin so convincingly displayed in the Abramoff story. The familiar deceit of sin is also displayed. Some of it is consciously perpetrated by the sinner, and some blinds the sinner with its layers of self-justification.

Another piece of high-quality journalism is a 2007 investigation by Debbie Cenziper in the *Miami Herald*. This article exposed the rampant corruption in public housing administration in Miami. Again, it is a story that illustrates the contours of structural and personal sin and the broad ripple effects of sin in full momentum. No area of human life is exempt from sin. The sheer inventiveness and persistence of corruption in public housing is a high irony: even the effort to provide safe and affordable housing for the poorest members of the community is tainted with greed.

Other areas of human life that touch the work of the pastor every day are also illuminated in the list of recent Pulitzer winners. *New York Times* writers Joseph Kahn and Jim Yardley won a journalism prize for their work on the ragged justice system in China. It is a story of success and failure, hope and despair. The poor farmer, the political dissenter, the urban factory worker—these are the ones crushed by a judicial system both antiquated and corrupt. Although a congregation is far different from an enormously populous country like China and the pastor not a ruthless judge, the basic dynamics of success and failure, hope and despair are often the dynamics in a local congregation as well. Although not as visibly dramatic, the currents and tides of human life in a congregation often reflect these same features of dispossessed and falsely imprisoned citizens in China. The pastor who is well-read in such literature will understand more deeply the human struggles in the congregation.

More than sin and struggle come to light in rich and vivid detail in these Pulitzer Prize winners. The work of *Rocky Mountain News* writer Jim Sheeler recounts the kindness and faithfulness of a Marine major who helps the families of those who have lost loved ones in Iraq. Here is a story that brims with the notes of the gospel.

The work of Nicholas Kristof of the *New York Times* illustrates the gospel theme of redemption. Although his editorials are often searing in their depiction of world crises, their very truth also reveals the hidden corners of hope. Kristof brings the world's worst atrocities to light and calls responsible citizens to political action. His editorials bring into the open the plight of young girls sold to sexual slavery in Indonesia, the persistence of female genital cutting in Africa, and the ongoing murder and rape in Darfur, to give three examples. These stories of suffering are painful, but they are sometimes marked by acts of sacrifice, courage, and faith. Kristof helps us understand the high but necessary cost of overcoming evil. His editorials offer a sober perspective on the cost of Christ's own sacrifice and courage for the sake of a wounded world.

Biography is another category in the Pulitzer Prizes that can also play a part in ongoing ministerial formation. The professional hazards and pitfalls of the life of the minister come into sharp focus in the 2006 biography by Debby Applegate, *The Most Famous Man in America: The Biography of Henry Ward Beecher*. The successes and influences of the nineteenth-century preacher, in his tireless work for the abolition of slavery and the rights of women, are set alongside the equally sensational failures of his marriage promises in a widely publicized adulterous affair. This juxtaposition of faithfulness in ministry, on the one hand, and a breach of marital fidelity, on the other, is a cautionary tale for pastors who face unique challenges in their leadership positions. A book such as Debby Applegate's will support that reflection.

Excellent newspaper journalism and biography are not the only components of a lifelong learning plan of reading for the pastor. Fiction and poetry can also contribute to the sustaining of pastoral ministry. Here, of course, the possibilities are virtually endless. Engaging and illuminating novels include Pulitzer Prize winners Marilynne Robinson's *Gilead* (2005), Richard Russo's *Empire Falls* (2002), and Toni Morrison's *Beloved* (1998). Many other contemporary novelists are especially suggestive when exploring the implications of grace in human communities. Wendell Berry's wonderful series of novels about the fictional but recognizable town of Port Williams is a rich and enjoyable collection that yields heartwarming and heartbreaking accounts of faith, perseverance, betrayal, grace, grief, hope, prayer, worship, and community. Port Williams is a landscape of pastoral imagination. *Jayber Crow*, *Hannah Coulter*, *The Memory of Old Jack*, and *Andy Catlett: Early Travels* are some of the novels in this series. Each breaks open in fresh and sometimes startling ways the issues that pastors deal with every day. My own understanding of living faithfully with the promises we make, promises that pull in their wake both joy and suffering, has forever been changed by a reading and then a rereading of *Jayber Crow*.

One of Berry's Port Williams narratives is a short story entitled "Pray without Ceasing," which is included in a four-volume anthology,

Listening for God: Contemporary Literature and the Life of Faith,
edited by Paula Carlson and Peter Hawkins.[1] In this story, Thad Coulter, a Port Williams resident and part of a prominent family, kills his
best friend in broad daylight on the main street of town because the
friend would not lend him a large sum of money. Thad is arrested and
jailed. Overcome by shame and horror, Thad sits in his jail cell and
longs for his own death. But he then receives a visitor, his daughter,
Martha Elizabeth. The narrator writes, "In that moment, he saw his
guilt included in love that stood as near him as Martha Elizabeth and
at that moment wore her flesh. . . . Surely God's love includes people
who can't bear it." The narrator of the story continues, "People sometimes talk of God's love as if it's a pleasant thing. But it is terrible, in
a way. Think of all it includes. It included Thad Coulter, mean and
drunk and foolish, before he killed Mr. Feltner, and it included him
afterwards." This expression of the wide inclusion of God's love in
grace and redemption takes on in this story flesh and blood, narrative,
texture, and content.

Although Wendell Berry does it impressively, many other novelists
also contribute to the sustaining of pastoral imagination and perception. The 1996 novel *The Rapture of Canaan* by Sheri Reynolds is
another story of a community, this one in transition and crisis. The
story is told of the fundamentalist Church of Fire and Brimstone and
God's Almighty Baptizing Wind. The community is thrown into a crisis when the fourteen-year-old granddaughter of the charismatic
leader of the church becomes pregnant by her teenaged prayer partner. The consequences of this are terrifying in the Fire and Brimstone
community. Much later, after painful events of rejection and punishment, the granddaughter finds a new place of hope and freedom. She
then reflects, "When I was a child, I saw our community as a special
place where God's special children could be safe from the influence
of the wicked world. Later, when I was older, I saw our community
differently. I saw us like an island. Like an island sinking from the
weight of fearful hearts."[2] Here the tenuous balance between discipline and freedom, tradition and exploration, law and gospel are ten-
tatively explored and mapped.

Other contemporary writers with an exceptional insight on human
life include Kent Haruf and Alice Munro. Kent Haruf's *Plainsong* and
Eventide are both crackling good novels with stories as hopeful and

heartbreaking as you will find. The two novels' take on grace and redemption is humane, often humorous, and finely characterized. Alice Munro, the Canadian master of short stories, splits open the realities of life, marriage, community, death, and illness like a chisel on a coconut. Her collections include *Lives of Girls and Women, Runaway,* and *Hateship, Friendship, Courtship, Loveship.* She captures in these short stories the connections and disruptions in human life that, although usually taking place in the vast Ontario interior a hundred years ago, feel real and present. Both Haruf and Monroe might be added to the pastor's list of reading.

A lifelong learning plan will include many other goals as well, all of which can contribute to a healthy and long life of pastoral ministry. But there is hardly a more enjoyable learning plan than the steady reading of wonderful novels and nonfiction. Both pastor, in sermon preparation and pastoral care, and congregation, in listening and discussing, will learn to spot the deep incarnational resemblances between the themes of the gospel and the themes of human experience and observation. The sustaining of pastoral ministry through reading will, in fact, support both pastor and people.

Notes

1. Paula Carlson and Peter S. Hawkins, *Listening for God: Contemporary Literature and the Life of Faith,* 4 vols. (Minneapolis: Augsburg Fortress Press, 1994–2003).
2. Sheri Reynolds, *The Rapture of Canaan* (New York: Berkley Books, 1996), 17.

28

Questions for the Preacher

DAWN OTTONI WILHELM

Ask a question—
> of God, Scripture, ourselves and this blessed but broken world.
> Then ask another.

For those who preach the gospel with the wild hope that somehow our words—our flawed, sometimes inconsistent, and always insufficient words—may open a way for us to love God and neighbors more fully, the best advice I can offer is to learn to ask questions. The art and craft of asking questions is as old as Scripture itself yet woefully unfamiliar to most twenty-first-century North Americans. Many people come to worship on Sunday morning with longings in their hearts and questions on their minds that they dare not speak aloud or have never learned to articulate. Countless others would rather avoid asking questions altogether or have chosen places of inquiry other than the church to raise their questions. Many others are so overwhelmed with life's hardships and injustices that they need someone else to raise questions on their behalf. For all of these (and for our own sakes also), we do what God in Christ has done for us: we go in search of others, with others. We enter fully into this world in search of God's world.

172

And because we are explorers more than mapmakers, we ask questions to discover Christ's way among us.

Two questions serve to guide this essay: What do questions do as we seek to fulfill the command to love God and neighbors? How do we ask questions that help us proclaim the gospel and engage others in the good news of Jesus Christ? Certainly, these are not the only questions worthy of our consideration. Neither is it possible to fully address them in the course of this brief essay. Yet the fact that I pose them reveals something about the priorities that govern my understanding and practice of preaching, which is one of the most important reasons to ask questions.

But first, a word of clarification. Asking questions is not a rhetorical trick to be manipulated into a new form of sermon design: I am not suggesting that we raise one question after another in the course of our sermons or that we always end with a question. I also resist the practice of asking questions for which "Jesus" is the assumed answer: God's love compels us to reach beyond rote expectations to enter unknown realms of love and suffering. Still less am I advocating a system of homiletical inquiry that exercises our intellects alone: the command to love God with all our heart, soul, mind, and strength demands the integration of these so that thought, action, spirituality, and human will become vital and necessary partners in the life of faith. Rather, I am advocating a way of questioning texts, God, ourselves, and the world around us so that our sermons will explore what troubles our minds, pulls at our heartstrings, challenges our assumptions, and propels us to participate in God's reign. I am proposing a theological and practical discipline that promotes honest inquiry and spiritual integrity as we attend to God's living presence and power among us. Just as preaching may be biblical without the reciting of one passage of Scripture after another, so may our sermons be guided by the questions we ask without our interrogating our listeners ad nauseam. The goal is to recognize and honor our most urgent questions, to do this in the company of God and others, and to appreciate that our doing so is perhaps the most profound act of worship we may offer to God and encourage in one another.

What do questions do as we seek to fulfill the command to love God and neighbors? Perhaps most obvious of all, questions presuppose that there is something we do not know about God, neighbors, ourselves, and the world around us. In his reflections on Socratic dialogue, Hans-Georg Gadamer describes "the logical structure of openness" that is necessary for genuine inquiry and the art of asking questions. If we think it is easier to ask questions than to answer them, if we only use dialogue to prove ourselves right rather than seek new insight, we are ignorant of our ignorance. "In order to be able to ask, one must want to know, which involves knowing that one does not know. . . . To ask a question is to bring it into the open."[1]

For those who are called to love God with heart, soul, mind, and strength, and our neighbors as ourselves, genuine inquiry demands the spiritual disposition of humility (acknowledging that there is something or someone we do not know) and attentiveness (holding open a place of mutual respect and receptivity). Beyond rendering opinions, confessing theological convictions, or offering spiritual insights, authentic inquiry assumes that none of us is the sole repository of divine wisdom, knowledge, and love. In order to cultivate this disposition of openness to others, we ask questions. We interrupt our internal monologue to invite friends, foes, strangers, and relatives into purposeful conversation. We ask questions of clarification so that our confusion does not grow into misunderstanding and resentment; we wonder aloud what it means when only a few people ask questions at congregational business meetings or when one item of business commands our attention more than others; we invite those whose voices have not been heard to share what they are thinking and then listen attentively to them. We confront the dual sins of arrogance and ignorance whenever we confess the inadequacy of our knowledge and become receptive to God and others.

Perhaps that is what questions do best of all: they draw us into conversation with God and others. They come *from* someone and are directed *to* someone. There is no surer way of ending a conversation or a relationship than refusing to answer another's question or to raise one of our own. God knows this and keeps raising questions with us as well. It is written into the fabric of Scripture itself: from the moment God and humanity experienced alienation from one another, God asked, "Where are you?" (Gen. 3:9). It is a question spoken by the One who seeks others, who freely speaks and carefully listens, who asks questions not because God is unknowing or unaware but because God longs to be in relationship with us. God's question reveals our self-imposed alienation and urges us to consider where we are in relationship to God. According to Abraham Joshua Heschel, "All of human history as described in the Bible may be summarized in one phrase: *God in search of man*."[2] We are not only called to love God with heart, soul, mind, and strength and our neighbors as ourselves, but God invites us to ask questions so that we may better know those whom we are called to love. This is not only a personal endeavor but an ethical one as well. In his book *Other-wise Preaching*, John McClure speaks of "the commitment to human others of all shapes and sizes and a personal and theological commitment to exiting the biblical, theological, social, experiential, and cultural hegemonies that exist within and beyond the churches."[3] Love calls us into relationships of responseability, and the questions we raise can move us beyond boundaries of our own making in anticipation of God's transforming work among us.

How do we ask questions that help us proclaim the gospel and engage others in the good news of Jesus Christ? We begin by recognizing that the openness of our questions is not boundless. The way we frame a question suggests a certain direction while excluding others.[4] For example, my first question—What do questions do as we seek to fulfill the command to love God and neighbors?—includes several presuppositions that guide us in a particular direction. It presupposes that questions are somehow related to religious faith and practice, that the dual commands of Deuteronomy 6:5 and Leviticus 19:18 (reiterated by Jesus in all four Gospels) are worthy priorities for Christian faith and the proclamation of the gospel, and that the two commands are necessarily related to one another. In other words, the horizon of openness suggested here is not limitless: it is bounded by a determination to pursue God's loving intentions for all people.[5] These presuppositions set us along a trajectory that is faithful to the gospel's priorities and essential to Christian preaching. My opening question assumes their import and guides our discussion.

In learning how to ask questions, we must acknowledge that those who ask questions exert a powerful influence over the course of our conversations. We may not know where our questions will lead us, but they command our attention by pointing us in a particular direction. A preacher who understood this particularly well was Walter Rauschenbusch. Although he cautioned ministers not to become the megaphone of political parties, he certainly urged them to "be the master of politics by creating the issues which parties will have to espouse. Questions are usually discussed a long time before they become political issues."[6] Inspired by gospel imperatives, Rauschenbusch knew the inherent privilege, potential, and responsibility that is given to pastors and preachers in deciding which questions to pursue and how to pursue them. If we want to learn how to ask questions, we must learn to appreciate the power inherent in them.

Given that questions point us in particular directions and those who raise questions exert a powerful influence over the course of our conversations, we would be wise to consider carefully what Jesus teaches us through his use of interrogatives. The many questions he raises in the Gospels indicate their importance for engaging others in God's reign. They also suggest patterns of inquiry that may guide our understanding of how to ask questions that encourage our love of God and neighbors.

In the Gospel of Luke alone, Jesus asks nearly eighty questions. To be sure, many of these serve rhetorical purposes as he assumes a particular answer (e.g., 2:49; 6:39; 13:15–16; 14:28). But from the time of his youth, Jesus asked questions of teachers in the Temple (2:49), and there is no doubt that questions were instrumental to his proclamation of God's reign. In typical rabbinic fashion, he often introduces his parables with a question, highlighting their importance and focusing our attention: "What is the kingdom of God like? And to what should I compare it?" (13:18). On other occasions, he asks questions to emphasize the ethical import of his teaching: "This very night your life is being demanded of you. And the things you have prepared, whose will they be?" (12:20). On still other occasions, his questions initiate significant teaching moments with his followers: "Who do the crowds say that I am? . . . But who do you say that I am?" (9:18–20). Questions also provoke his hearers to consider more deeply the certainty of God's justice: "And will not God grant justice to his chosen ones who cry to him day and night? . . . When the Son of Man comes, will he find faith on earth?" (18:7–8). After the resurrection, Jesus continues to raise questions as a way of engaging his followers on the road to Emmaus and as he meets them in Jerusalem (24:17, 19, 41). Like the Hebrew prophets before him (e.g., Isa. 5:4; Hos. 6:3–6; Mic. 6:6–8), Jesus raises questions to redirect our attention to God's priorities, concerns, and intentions for our lives, inviting our participation in God's reign.

Jesus' questions also teach us the importance of questioning injustice, sorrow, and pain. Many of them reflect intense frustration (Mark 8:17–21), personal agony (14:37, 41), and even abandonment by God (15:34). They reveal his compassion for sinners (Matt. 9:2–8), his interest in outsiders (Mark 5:30), and his determination to uncover hardness of heart among those who deny God's mercy to others (Mark 3:4). Jesus' questions not only point to the promise of God's reign but also to what is most troublesome and painful among us. In this way, he invites us to recognize and offer to God whatever questions arise out of our own experiences of suffering, betrayal, personal failure, systemic injustice, and the evil forces that threaten us. In his memoirs, Elie Wiesel insists, "Man is defined by what troubles him, not by what reassures him."[7] If we want to speak a gospel word that genuinely engages others, we must give voice to the unspoken questions that beg our attention. In this way, our questions not only acknowledge the reality of suffering, but they probe its inner recesses in search of hidden light.

We ask questions not only for our own sake but also for the sake of others—those who are afraid to ask questions, whose voices have been silenced by fear and oppression. For those who have never learned to ask questions for themselves and for all "others" we are called to love and serve, we ask questions. As leaders of corporate worship and ministers of the gospel of Jesus Christ, we are in the unique position to help create communities of inquiry, which resist premature closure on our attempts to understand and love others. More than conversation, we seek transformation, and we do so through worship and the questions we ask. As we seek to love both God and neighbor, our questions open a way for God's presence and power to move among us.

Notes

1. Hans-Georg Gadamer, *Truth and Method*, 2nd revised ed., trans. and rev. Joel Weinsheimer and Donald G. Marshall (New York: Continuum, 2004), 357.
2. Abraham Joshua Heschel, *God in Search of Man: A Philosophy of Judaism* (New York: Farrar, Straus & Giroux, 1980), 136.
3. John S. McClure, *Other-wise Preaching: A Postmodern Ethic for Homiletics* (St. Louis: Chalice Press, 2001), 133–34.
4. Gadamer is helpful in reminding us that there are false questions (those that are not truly open to another's response) and slanted questions (those that

intend an openness but remain unaware of the presuppositions governing them). He insists that a question "has been put wrongly when it does not reach the state of openness but precludes reaching it by retaining false presuppositions. It pretends to an openness and susceptibility to decision that it does not have." Similarly, he calls "slanted" a question that "has deviated from the right direction. The slant of a question consists in the fact that it does not give any real direction, and hence no answer to it is possible." Gadamer, *Truth and Method*, 357–58.

5. Here we may recall Augustine's teaching: "Whoever, therefore, thinks that he understands the divine Scriptures or any part of them so that it does not build the double love of God and of our neighbor does not understand it at all." Saint Augustine, *On Christian Doctrine*, trans. D. W. Robertson Jr. (Upper Saddle, NJ: Prentice-Hall, 1958), 30.

6. Walter Rauschenbusch, *Christianity and the Social Crisis in the 21st Century: The Classic That Woke Up the Church*, ed. Paul Rauschenbusch (New York: Harper One, 2007), 295. On the hundredth anniversary of the publication of Rauschenbusch's classic work, this volume includes his treatise as well as essays by contemporary Christian scholars, preachers, and activists.

7. Elie Wiesel, *Memoirs: All Rivers Run to the Sea* (New York: Schocken Books, 1995), 124.

29

My Advice for Preachers

WILLIAM H. WILLIMON

It's About God

Preaching that is Christian is talk about God, talk engendered by the peculiar God who has commandeered Israel and the church for God's loving purposes with the world. Alas, much of the preaching that I hear is mostly advice. At its best, the advice given is relatively valuable advice. Yet it is little different from the advice that one could receive anywhere else. The line between church and Rotary gets thin, and Rotary at least meets at a convenient hour of the week and serves lunch!

Preaching that is boring is preaching that talks first about us and then only tangentially about God. Preaching that is faithful is preaching that talks first about God and then only secondarily and derivatively talks about us. The God of Scripture is so much more interesting than we are. We are in great need of theological refurbishment of preaching that rescues us from the essentially anthropological captivity of much contemporary preaching.

Scripture gives preachers something interesting to say. Preaching will be invigorated in a recovery of the Bible as a talking book. It's good news for us preachers that the criticism of Scripture has moved from essentially historical concerns to literary interests. We preachers resonate to the ways in which biblical writers present the truth of Jesus Christ through a wide array of artistic and literary devices.

When I entered the pastoral ministry, I thought my great homiletical challenge was how to talk with modern, skeptical, critical people about the naive, premodern world of the Bible. Now I believe that our great challenge is to sort through the assorted contemporary spiritualities at work in the marketplace and, in our sermons, raise the question "Which God are you talking about?"

That's a challenge for me as a mainline, liberal Protestant. The great theological project of our segment of Christendom has been intellectual accommodation, adjustment, and assimilation of the biblical God to the modern world. Particularities, distinctions, and oddities of the God of Israel and the church were seen as a threat to communication with modern people. I now believe that the peculiar God who is rendered in Scripture is the best hope we have of getting a hearing among relentlessly spiritual, postmodern people who are confused about which gods are true and which are false.

Good Preachers Are Great Readers

I've never known a good writer who was not a great reader. The same is true for preachers. Preachers attempt to raise the dead, move the world, birth the church, and offer Christ with nothing but words. Yet we preach in a culture that cheapens speech, and I'm not only talking about George W. Bush's abuse of the language. Most of our public discourse is dominated by the speech of advertising.

I, therefore, keep two or three books going. I read not only for substance, for argument and ideas, but rather for words. It is invigorating to spend time with people who love language and use it well.

In my old age, I'm reading more poetry, more fiction (which is usually more true than nonfiction) and less contemporary theology. I'm demoralized enough without being further discouraged by the latest theological take on this or that. The best of poetry and fiction take the long view, deal in an immediate way with only the most important matters, and want to be in conversation with more than academia. Good writing has a way of pruning my speech and strengthening my skills. Words are the only tools of a preacher. We must keep our tools in good shape.

I am concerned that the use of PowerPoint and other visual media may further degrade our ability to use words to communicate the gospel. The gospel is an inherently acoustical matter. Faith comes through hearing. There are those who believe that in an electronic, visual culture, people will only relate to the visual, not the verbal. I have a different take on this. I believe that if language is degraded, as fewer public figures have the gifts and the training to use language well, there is a sense in which we preachers will find the world offering us the gift of a new hearing. The simple wonder of one human being standing up and speaking to other human beings will again become miraculous. Having been conned so often by slick, manipulative, quick-fix artists on TV, people will once again be filled with wonder at the joy of hearing someone stand up and testify.

The Power of Imitation

This is my advice for new and developing preachers. Imitate! Preaching is an art, a craft, and like any other craft, you can't learn it from books, even books like this one! You must apprentice with a master craftsperson, look over the master's shoulder, watch how the master deals with the medium and works with the material, and get the feel of the craft. In classical rhetoric, the student studied and memorized the speeches of the masters for a dozen years before attempting to make any speeches of his own. The purpose of this listening is not to swipe the illustrations and ideas of another preacher, but rather to develop the skills needed to work up our own illustrations and ideas in our preaching.

Eventually, the developing preacher must discover his or her own voice, but that doesn't seem to happen until a preacher has thoroughly inculcated and internalized the voice of another. I recommend you study enough preachers to really get a feel for how a preacher works, then focus upon the work of two or three experienced preachers.

The goal of this observation and study is not slavish imitation but rather to get into the mind of a preacher, to discover the pitfalls and the weaknesses within an experienced preacher's way with the text. A self-assured, experienced preacher gives a less experienced preacher confidence, the willingness to risk and venture out in preaching, which is one of the greatest challenges for the new preacher.

On my iPod I can regularly listen to the sermons of a dozen different preachers. Just a generation ago no preacher ever got to hear the sermons of another preacher. Today, any preacher can study under the masters of the art.

Preparing to Preach

As I travel about, speaking with fellow pastors about the preaching task, someone inevitably asks, "How do you go about preparing your sermon?" It's a fair question. There is a sense in which any preacher worth his or her salt is always preparing a sermon. Nothing is ever wasted on a preacher. Experiences, even the worst of them, all provide grist for the creative preacher's mill. The most ethically formative aspect of being a pastor is disciplining your life and your schedule in such a way that you have a sermon ready for Sunday.

I find it helpful always to keep with me some means of jotting down ideas, impressions, and illustrations. Computer search programs enable the preacher to do a word search and to retrieve a previously collected illustration. One of the major tasks of the pastor is to help the faithful make connections between their everyday lives in the world and their Christian commitments. Therefore, when we preachers collect potential sermon illustrations, we are only doing that which is at the heart of all pastoral work—helping people make connections.

I don't work well under pressure. No "Saturday Night Specials" for me. I try to set aside a day every few months to begin work on my future sermons. I make a file folder for a given Sunday. I read aloud the lectionary texts for a future Sunday. Then I write down immediate impressions. I've learned to trust first impressions more than I used to. Your congregation may be encountering the biblical text for the first time. You do not want your first impressions to get lost in a mass of subsequent study and preparation.

In seminary, the biblical study that I was taught told us not to trust our first impressions. Go to the experts, the biblical commentators, who will tell you the correct, authoritative interpretation of a biblical text. I now feel differently. You are the preacher who is also the pastor. In your hands, the biblical text is in its native habitat. Scripture is for the edification and correction of the congregation, not for the amusement of an academic interpreter. In your pastoral work, the important questions are being raised for which the sermon based on the biblical text is the response.

Tom Long, one of our best instructors in these matters, says that the biblical preacher goes to the biblical text hoping to make a discovery. Then the preacher announces that discovery to the congregation. For Long, the preaching task is "front loaded." Most of the really interesting work occurs early in the preaching task, in the preacher's initial encounters with the biblical text. The preacher hopes to make some invigorating discovery that demands to be shared with the congregation. Discoveries are interesting; commonplace conventional wisdom is boring. If we are engaged by a discovery, we will find a way to share that discovery with the congregation. And we will not want our early discovery in working with the biblical text to be deflated by subsequent study with the "experts."

I then allow my thoughts to germinate in the succeeding weeks in my pastoral duties and in my continuing struggle with the biblical text. If I get some illustration, some insight or question, I drop it into the folder. My hope is that the sermon will continue to germinate and develop so that, when it comes time for me to write it, I'll have something that has had time to develop without the creative edges of my ideas becoming dulled by the process.

What I'm trying to do in this process is to keep as open as possible, to prevent anxiety about the hangman's noose facing me next Sunday from circumventing the imaginative process. I should not be surprised that in the normal round of pastoral interaction with people, some of the best biblical insights arise. The texts of the New Testament came into being in the first place in response to the faith questions of real Christians attempting to live out their faith in their daily lives and real pastors attempting to form the Christian community in their parishes.

The Centrality of Preaching

A concluding observation: preaching is the most important thing that we pastors do. In the last century, in our culture, we pastors have undertaken so many tasks—fund-raising, organizational management, leadership, counseling, community involvement. It is all too easy for the disciplines of preaching—prayer, study, self-reflection, reading, and writing—to get crowded out of our schedules. Luther's favorite designation for us pastors was "servants of the Word." In preaching we are engaged in the most definitive of pastoral tasks. The theological bases of our ministry are made explicit, the theological rationale for the church is refurbished, and we interact with the theological commitments that constitute and convene the church in the first place.

For some decades now, a number of commentators have devalued preaching, claiming that it is authoritarian, one-way communication, that it can't compete with the flashy, visual quality of the electronic media, that we ordinary preachers appear rather lame when compared with the media entertainers and communicators. Still, when asked what quality they most value in a pastor, right at the top or near the top, congregations always respond, "preaching."

In fact, in a media-saturated culture, the joy of a person standing up and testifying to the faith may be coming back. In a church always imperiled by theological amnesia, a loss of its theological focus, and assimilation into worldly expectations of success, preaching is that which helps the church maintain its identity as the church of Jesus Christ.

30

Loving a Peculiar People

STEVEN TOSHIO YAMAGUCHI

I f you are considering the plunge into the ministry as the preacher for a congregation, then I have two urgent appeals for you. First, cherish those peculiar people and be the faithful steward of their peculiar story. Listen expectantly and respectfully. Second, mine your peculiar place deeply and diligently. This kind of well-focused attention can open your study of Scripture to a bountiful treasure as you preach God's gospel to your congregation.[1]

God has called you and placed you in a particular spot on the earth. This is your particular place, your spot of holy ground unlike any other. Sometimes a neighbor's spot appears to have richer soil, fewer rocks, more water, a nicer view, and so forth. God has also called you to a peculiar people. They may at first glance seem similar to other people you have known or heard about. But this group of people is unique, and you are uniquely called to love and cherish them. To take this seriously is to enter a world of divine new possibilities.

David Hansen is a pastor, author, lifelong friend, and an encouragement to me in times of doubt. One of his stories changed the way I viewed my peculiar pastoral call during a difficult time. We were talking about his call to a yoked parish south of Missoula, Montana, near the Bitterroot Valley, not far from where Noman Maclean's *A River Runs Through It* takes place. When Dave first arrived in Montana he found himself in a fly fisher's paradise—the kind of place where fishing tourists will pay thousands of dollars for a few days of guided fishing, the kind of place that makes a fly fisher drop her jaw at the sight and revel in the glory of the rapturous, rushing beauty. These were Dave's spots to stop and fish on his way home from regular pastoral visits. He could have a stream like this all to himself all day long. His fishing was world class, and many of us envied his good fortune. People from around the world came to catch fish in those blue-ribbon trout streams. But the rich fishing became too familiar. The tourist's type of thrill waned. Meanwhile, Dave lived on the bank of a little stretch of river (relatively less spectacular) that he had not yet fished with success. (I tried to fish it, unsuccessfully.) He dedicated himself to that stretch of the river. It took many seasons before he began to catch fish expertly. Over the years he learned the seasons and the changes and the particularities of his little stretch of stream. Nobody else could fish that water like he could because he decided to learn everything he could as deeply as possible about his little spot. He told me, and I believe him, that it was more gratifying, in a different and deeper way, to connect with his own quirky fish than to catch the popular trophy fish on those famous tourist-destination streams.

This deep satisfaction in plumbing the peculiar waters that God had given him became a parable of his pastoral ministry in his peculiar spot of holy ground. You as the pastor can become the expert at connecting with your own quirky flock. It is your calling. Know them better than anyone else. This helps you care for them like no one else. You, uniquely, can help them become all that God wants them to be. You can preach for them like nobody else. But first you must cherish your peculiar congregation. You have to believe that you are the pastor God chose for them and they are the people whom God chose for you. This can be more difficult when someone else's "fishing spot" seems to yield more fish than years. (Sometimes those fishing stories are truly "fishy.")

Part of what makes a local fishing guide effective is that she knows the peculiar diet, environment, and habits of the local fish better than a nonlocal. Many an eager fly fisher approaches a new stream laden with a vest full of flies and gear that the fly fishing shop back home and the glossy fishing catalogs and TV fishing shows suggested he needs. But all of that paraphernalia might be for naught. The local expert can do better with a select handful of custom flies (which may look ugly) that she tied specifically to match the cuisine and fancy of her peculiar fish. If the local expert recommends her own peculiar fly, I will choose it every time over a beautiful store-bought textbook version. When tying her own flies, the local expert knows which materials to use for her peculiar fish. The stuff she chooses might be unconventional and result in nothing like the beautiful paradigmatic flies for sale at the fly shop, but the local expert knows best what "her fish" hanker for.

Studying Scripture for preaching can be similar. If you are the local expert, you can do the best deep, hard work. As local expert guide, you can make better choices than a nonlocal commenting from somewhere else. Preaching magazines, online sermon sources, even commentaries, can tempt like beautiful store-bought flies, but they rarely work as well as my own handmade version of the text. My Hebrew professor, Gordon Hugenberger, explained it like this (and it changed my life): When I am exegeting Samuel, I may zero in on a very interesting passage that seems peculiarly relevant to my congregation but is not mentioned in my commentaries. Have I missed the point? Consider this: The commentator on Samuel is given limited pages and only paid for so much time. The publisher can't sell a bloated tome where every interesting rabbit trail is explored. Commentators try to cover the high points; they can't dig into areas peculiar to your congregation as deeply as you can. Commentators cannot know your people like you do. A commentator might live in a world very different from yours. I find that this is even more significant for pastors who serve churches that are culturally (maybe linguistically, ethnically, or economically) very different from that of a commentator. If you listen well and pay careful attention to your peculiar people, you can become the local expert who lovingly selects what will best entice and feed your people with the gospel.

At the very time when Dave Hansen was getting acquainted with the idiosyncrasies of his wild and fishy neighbors, I was called to a different kind of wilderness. In 1988 God called me to serve as the pastor for Grace Presbyterian Church in Paramount, California. Chartered in 1925 as the Japanese Presbyterian Church of Long Beach, the church fled to neighboring Paramount in 1987. Average worship attendance was twenty-five. Most were retirees. Young people were gone. The building was ramshackle and dilapidated. The lawn was dead, flower beds were full of weeds, pew Bibles and hymnals had been vandalized, and the building was home to lots of vermin and church detritus. It had been five years since the church had baptized someone, so they hadn't noticed the baptismal font was missing. The church was on Compton Boulevard just east of Compton during the boom of crack cocaine and gang warfare. This peculiar congregation was shaken and shaky. I came fresh from Princeton Seminary with my Latin diploma and special awards, and I became the entire church staff at Grace. Meanwhile my buddy, Dave, was fishing pristine trout streams in Montana. Over the years we have realized that we were both doing the same pastoral thing.

As sad as Grace's circumstances were, the saddest of all struck me between the eyes when I stood in the pulpit after two weeks. I already knew most of the people, since thirteen (of the average twenty-five in worship) were on the Pastor Nominating Committee. But that Sunday I looked into their faces, and it struck me that most of them had been incarcerated by their own government and evacuated to concentration camps in the wilderness during World War II. By listening, I discovered that the church had never made explicit connections between their own story of wilderness exile and God's story in the Bible. I soon began preaching about exodus and wilderness and exile. We mined Scripture to see how a journey that appeared to outsiders to be God-forsaken was in fact not that at all. With our peculiar ears we listened to the Bible's stories of how God meets the people in the wilderness, journeys with, leads, and provides for them in the wilderness, and in the wilderness makes them into God's own peculiar people.

It was time for peculiar work. I fired up my Hebrew skills and did my exegesis as diligently as I was able in the context of getting to know this peculiar people. I discovered alternate renderings that commentators did not mention but that made great sense to the people. I had to dig harder, excavating unturned ground, because I was making decisions about the text that I didn't find in commentaries or preaching aids. As a growing steward of the people's story, doing diligent exegesis, I could help the people make their idiosyncratic connections to God's story. So even if we were a people in what felt like wilderness, and even if we were a people whose history had seemed God-forsaken, nevertheless we began to see our story woven into God's story, and we began to believe more confidently that God was present with us still. Our story became thankful and hopeful. Our people welcomed other kinds of wilderness refugees and exiles—from different nations, from the poor streets, from places of privilege and pain. Together we were growing into the peculiar people God called us to be. We could have been tempted to mimic other peculiar peoples, as we were surrounded by world-famous megachurches. Had we tried to be someone else, we would have starved and died. As the pastor, all I could do was take seriously this people's peculiar story in light of the authentic treasure God had in store for them in Scripture.

Now please heed this warning: *Do the hard work, but don't make a show of it.* The Hebrew and Greek exegesis I did (and still try to do) was harder than what I did in seminary. But the people didn't need to know that. To help us understand this, Bryant Kirkland told us in his Princeton preaching class (which also changed my life) that if you are a skilled cabinet maker and you make a jewelry box for your beloved, when the gift is finished, you should just give the gift, then be quiet. Let the beauty and art speak for themselves. He explained that too many preachers show off their tools. They take you into their garage to admire their expensive German chisels, and they show you the wood shavings and the hand-selected wood grains that they didn't use—all before presenting the gift to their beloved. Just give the gift! Even when I have the Hebrew or Greek text before me in the pulpit, I do not flaunt the common phrase "In the original Greek . . ." That exclusive phrase can disempower the people by suggesting that real meaning is inscrutable to them and only the pastor can really decipher it. Too many preachers use this haughty phrase only to offer a simplistic or even mistaken use of the Greek cursorily lifted from a commentary. (But it puts the people in their place.) There are artful and humble ways to present the beauty of a genuinely hard-earned gift without slipping into geeky, off-putting techno-talk about your fancy chisels and custom glues. After a year of this difficult preaching, one venerated elder said to me, "I like your sermons because they're not so theological." I grinned and hoped I knew what he meant—that my preaching wasn't littered by geeky, theological technicalities. I believe it was deeply theological preaching shaped by excruciating exegesis. But it wasn't about my hard work. It was all about presenting the simple, beautiful gift of the good news of God's story intersecting the peculiar story of this peculiar people.

We found the baptismal font (buried beneath the church detritus) and restored it. In the fifth year, our older daughter, Lydia, was one of four baptized in August. In the eighth year, our younger daughter, Joy, was one of twenty-five baptized on Easter Sunday. Grace outgrew its old building, moved, merged with another congregation, and is now part of a dynamic, missional, multicultural congregation called Grace First Presbyterian Church.

This is difficult work, but whose pastoral work isn't? It is sometimes terrifying, and sometimes it feels like we are strangely lost. But we are never alone. We are bound to a peculiar people on a particular mission with the living God in our midst leading the way. Who would want to miss the joy of witnessing God's glory on such a peculiar journey?

Note

1. I refer to "your" congregation guardedly. A pastor might rightly refer to "my church" just as any member might refer to "my church"—because it is a place where one belongs, not a thing that one possesses. Because "my congregation" coming from a pastor's lips can suggest possessiveness rather than belongingness, I prefer referring to "the congregation I serve" rather than "my congregation." So I refer to "your congregation" remembering that congregations are God's possessions that you and I are privileged to serve.

Contributors

Joanna M. Adams
Senior Pastor, Morningside Presbyterian Church, Atlanta

Ronald J. Allen
Nettie Sweeney and Hugh Th. Miller Professor of Preaching and New Testament, Christian Theological Seminary, Indianapolis

Craig Barnes
Robert Meneilly Professor of Leadership and Ministry, Pittsburgh Theological Seminary, and Senior Pastor, Shadyside Presbyterian Church, Pittsburgh

David Bartlett
Professor of New Testament, Columbia Theological Seminary, Decatur, Georgia

John Buchanan
Senior Pastor, Fourth Presbyterian Church, Chicago, and Editor and Publisher of the *Christian Century*

David G. Buttrick
Drucilla Moore Buffington Professor of Homiletics and Liturgics, Emeritus, Vanderbilt Divinity School, Nashville

William J. Carl III
President and Professor of Homiletics, Pittsburgh Theological Seminary, Pittsburgh, and Former Senior Pastor, First Presbyterian Church, Dallas

Jana Childers
Dean of the Seminary and Professor of Homiletics and Speech Communication, San Francisco Theological Seminary, San Anselmo, California

Fred B. Craddock
Bandy Distinguished Professor of Preaching and New Testament, Emeritus, Candler School of Theology at Emory University, Atlanta

191

Miguel A. De La Torre
Associate Professor of Social Ethics, Iliff School of Theology, Denver

Katharine Rhodes Henderson
Executive Vice President, Auburn Theological Seminary, New York

James C. Howell
Senior Pastor, Myers Park United Methodist Church, Charlotte, North Carolina

Mary Lin Hudson
Professor of Homiletics and Liturgics, Memphis Theological Seminary, Memphis, Tennessee

Cleophus J. LaRue
Francis Landy Patton Associate Professor of Homiletics, Princeton Theological Seminary, Princeton, New Jersey

Michael L. Lindvall
Senior Pastor, Brick Presbyterian Church, New York

Thomas G. Long
Bandy Professor of Preaching, Candler School of Theology at Emory University, Atlanta

Jennifer Lord
Associate Professor of Homiletics and Dean of the Chapel, Austin Presbyterian Theological Seminary, Austin, Texas

John S. McClure
Charles G. Finney Professor of Homiletics and Chair, Graduate Department of Religion, Vanderbilt Divinity School, Nashville

Alyce M. McKenzie
Associate Professor of Homiletics, Perkins School of Theology at Southern Methodist University, Dallas

Earl Palmer
Senior Pastor, University Presbyterian Church, Seattle

Eugene Peterson
Pastor Emeritus, Christ Our King Presbyterian Church, Bel Air, Maryland, and Professor Emeritus of Spiritual Theology, Regent College, Vancouver, British Columbia

Hyung Cheon Rim
Senior Pastor, Young Nak Presbyterian Church, Los Angeles

Joseph L. Roberts Jr.
Senior Pastor, Historic Ebenezer Baptist Church, Atlanta

Marguerite Shuster
Harold John Ockenga Professor of Preaching and Theology, Fuller Theological Seminary, Pasadena, California

Gardner Taylor
Senior Pastor Emeritus, Concord Baptist Church, Brooklyn, New York, and Distinguished Visiting Professor, Shaw University Divinity School, Raleigh, North Carolina

Thomas H. Troeger
J. Edward and Ruth Cox Lantz Professor of Christian Communication, Yale Divinity School, New Haven, Connecticut

Leanne Van Dyk
Dean and Vice President of Academic Affairs and Professor of Reformed Theology, Western Theological Seminary, Holland, Michigan

Dawn Ottoni Wilhelm
Associate Professor of Preaching and Worship, Bethany Theological Seminary, Richmond, Indiana

William H. Willimon
Bishop, United Methodist Church, North Alabama Conference, Birmingham, and Former Dean of the Chapel, Duke University, Durham, North Carolina

Steven Toshio Yamaguchi
Executive Presbyter, Presbytery of Los Ranchos (PCUSA), Southern California, and former Senior Pastor, Grace Presbyterian Church, Long Beach, California